POTBOILER
An Amateur's Affair with La Cuisine

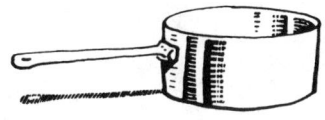

ROBERT CANZONERI

North Point Press   San Francisco   1989

Copyright © 1989 by Robert Canzoneri
Printed in the United States of America

I am grateful to the following for material I have quoted or have used in somewhat altered form as credited at appropriate places in the text.

A Man's Taste. The Junior League of Memphis, Inc., Memphis, Tennessee (1980).

Helen Brown, *Helen Brown's West Coast Cook Book*. Little, Brown & Company, Boston (1952). (Copyright 1952 by Helen Evans Brown.)

Auguste Escoffier, *Le Guide Culinaire*. Translated by H. L. Craknell and R. J. Kaufmann. Mayflower Books, New York. (Copyright Flammarion 1921 by Flammarion.)

Auguste Escoffier, *Ma Cuisine*. Translated by Vyvyan Holland. A & W Publishers, New York (1978). (Copyright Ernest Flammarion 1934; copyright English text, The Hamlyn Publishing Group Limited, 1965.)

Theodora Fitzgibbon, *A Taste of Rome*. Houghton Mifflin Company, Boston (1975). (Copyright 1975 by Theodora Fitzgibbon.)

Gourmet, October 1984. Copyright 1984 by The Condé Nast Publications, Inc.

Ladies of Lynchburg Recipes. Lynchburg, Tennessee. (Copyright [no date] Lynchburg Hardware and General Store.)

Stephen Leacock, *Laugh with Leacock*. Dodd, Mead & Company, New York.

All epigraphs are quoted from Stephen Leacock's "Gertrude the Governess" with the generous permission of Barbara Nimmo, executrix of the Leacock estate, and of Dodd, Mead and Company.

Memphis Cookbook. The Junior League of Memphis, Inc., Memphis, Tennessee (1952, 1980).

Monica Sheridan, *The Art of Irish Cooking*. Gramercy, New York (1965). (Copyright 1965 by Monica Sheridan.)

Sue Style, *Larousse Mexican Cookbook*. Larousse & Co., New York (1984). (Copyright Sue Style 1984.)

Woman's Exchange Cook Book. The Woman's Exchange of Memphis, Inc., Memphis, Tennessee (1964, 1967).

The section entitled "Mayonnaise" was published in somewhat different form in *Southern Magazine*, February 1987.

In addition to those mentioned with some prominence in the text, I'd like to thank the following for encouragement and suggestions: Bill, Carey, Ernest, Hillary, Hugh, Jim, Kate, Linda, Michael, and Roberta.

LIBRARY OF CONGRESS CATALOGING-IN-PUBLICATION DATA
Canzoneri, Robert.
    Potboiler : an amateur's affair with la cuisine.
    Includes index.
    1. Cookery.   I. Title.
TX714.C36   1989   641.5   88-34574
ISBN 0-86547-360-9

For P. Rat, Bear, Topper, and Irene

Contents

I. WAS THIS THE DAWN OF LOVE? ... 3
  1. Where I Cook and What I Cook For ... 5
    Steak and Potatoes ... 8
    Cannelloni ... 9
    Pizza ... 12
  2. Escoffier, Je Suis Ici ... 16
    French Bread ... 20

II. THE MEETING ... 23
  3. La Cuisine, C'est Moi ... 25
    Beef Stroganoff Irene ... 30
    Beef Bourguignon ... 32
    Hollandaise Sauce ... 35
  4. By the Book ... 36

III. SETTLING IN ... 41
  5. Not Yet the Hollandaise, Too Soon the Game Hens ... 43
    Marge's Tomato Juice ... 48
    Bloody Marys ... 49
    Crabmeat Justine ... 51

Rock Cornish Game Hens with Pine Nut Stuffing	53
6. Allegro, Ma Non Troppo	55
Stir-Frying	59
The Jewels of Mei Tang Poo	62
Confusion Blossoms in the New Year	64
IV. VIGIL 'NEATH THE CASEMENT	67
7. Upstaged	69
Upstaged Menu	75
Chilled Consommé Madrilène	76
Suprêmes de Volaille à la Bordelaise	77
Salade Verte	79
Pêches Melba	81
8. The Pasta Machine	83
Making Pasta	87
Fettuccine Alfredo	89
Pasta Impressionista	91
Spaghetti San Remo	93
Spaghetti Carbonara	94
Spaghetti Balduini	95
Ravioli	97
Lasagne	99
V. THE DAYS PASS SWIFTLY	103
9. The Back Fence	105
Bob's Roast, Modified	112
Ken's Chinese Barbecued Ribs	114
Ice Cream	116
VI. ANTECEDENTS	121
10. Still Farther Back	123
Mom's Rolls	131
Albino Spaghetti	134

Fig Preserves	136
Potatoes on the Half Shell	138
Turnip Greens, Field Peas, and Cornbread	139
Grandmomma's Ginger Snaps	142
Mom's Lemon Meringue Pie	145

VII. FROM HUMBLE BEGINNINGS	149
11. The Shriek of Celery	151
12. That Depression Mentality	154
Barbecue	158
Slaw	161
Candy's Baked Beans	163

VIII. COMING THROUGH	165
13. Waste Not, Want Not	167
Suprêmes de Volaille en Papillote	173
Boning	178
Soup from Stock	180

IX. CALM BEFORE THE STORM	183
14. A Cabinet Named Harry	185
Mayonnaise	189
Yolks and Whites	193
Soufflés	195
Quiche Irene	198
Augusta National Quiche	200

X. THE PLOT THICKENS	203
15. Others, Lord Yes, Others	205
Mexican Food	208
16. "Did I Catch You at a Bad Time?"	216
Omelettes	221
Filet Mignon Poulet	223
Coffee	225

XI. IN SPITE OF ALL · 227

17. Liver? Never! · 229
Mock Bahama-Bound Black Bean Soup · 234
Spaghetti Caruso · 236
Pasta with a Guilty Secret · 238
Plaid Zucchini · 240
Chunky Dry Chicken Pie · 242
Suprêmes de Volaille Peanut Butter and Horseradish · 243

XII. DÉNOUEMENT · 245

18. From Mary to Martha · 247
Wild Bill's Chili · 252
Wild Bill's Pot Roast · 254
Tom's Country Ham · 255
Cheese Grits · 256

XIII. CODA · 259

19. A Womb with a View · 261
20. La Cucina È Mobile · 264
Hamburgers · 270
Skewering · 272
Louie's Chicken and Andouille Gumbo · 274
Louie's Crawfish Étouffée · 277

XIV. SILVER LINING · 279

21. Where Does It All Go? · 281

INDEX · 285

POTBOILER

I

Was This the Dawn of Love?

"The two were destined to meet.
Nearer and nearer they came.
And then still nearer."

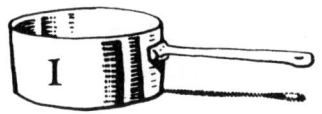

Where I Cook and What I Cook For

Thoreau said that one reason he went out to Walden Pond was to back life into a corner. One reason I spend a lot of time in a little kitchen on a tiny cul-de-sac in the small town of Westerville, Ohio, is that life sort of backed me into a corner.

The things that brought me to this particular kitchen, and started me cooking, coalesced some eleven or twelve years ago when Candy and I bought this house for Mr. Micawber, our Old English sheepdog. We ourselves had coalesced a couple of years earlier: Candy from sorority-house life as an undergraduate and then from efficiency-apartment living as a graduate student; I from twenty-odd years of teaching around the country and of being cooked for along with a couple of growing children. We started out in a no-pets second-floor apartment; when Micawber arrived, we moved into a duplex (known around here as a "twin single") and launched a real estate agent on a long search for just the right house—a good-sized fenced or fenceable yard, lots of trees, lots of windows, no basement, no upstairs, no needless space to clean.

We bought this house because it was even better than we'd hoped for, not realizing what it would do to our lives. For one thing, there was something about having a kitchen all our own just sitting there, waiting. The rest of the house, and the yard around it, drew Candy; she began a miniature jungle indoors—a Norfolk pine, a tall corn plant, philodendrons, massive ferns, a rubber plant, dumb cane—and set to digging flower beds outside. But for me the kitchen was like a vacuum that had to be filled. Now it seems as though I was virtually sucked in all at once, but retrospect is deceptive; the fact is that I was suckered in a step at a time and had to fight for every single uncertain foothold.

I had cooked before, though I was far from being a cook. In my former existence, in fact, I somehow heard about herbs and invented a pizza sauce that used pretty near every kind the supermarket had to offer and left your mouth tingly for days. Considerably later, while we were in that second-floor apartment, I was forced into the kitchen, briefly, again. Candy had furiously scribbled notes as Julia Child performed a rather elaborate Gallic pot roast, and then had set about to do it herself, for company. But she got sick at the last minute and left it for me to finish. I have a vague impression that the dinner turned out very well. What I had to do to finish the pot roast, though, I must have been too traumatized to record in memory. Perhaps I just took it off the stove.

Later still, in the twin single, I made up my own version of cannelloni. I should have expected bad luck with cannelloni. Not long before, we had gone to a fake Italian restaurant where they greeted us with something like "Bony Sarah," and I got so excited that I tried to order in my own quasi Italian. "*Due* cannelloni," I told the waitress grandly, holding up two fingers. She grasped her little order pad before her in both hands and answered in nasal Ohioan, "Yes, we do."

But my own cannelloni turned out just great, for the two of us. I made the pasta myself and decided that it was best not cooked in boiling water first but rolled raw around the filling and baked so with a rather piquant (all those herbs again) tomato sauce.

Of course, arrogance got the better of me and I tried making the cannelloni for company. I had been impressed several years earlier—dazzled, really—at dinner with my friends Nancy and Murray when Nancy brought out course after course of Chinese food she had made by hand. She would be the first to witness what *I* could do, now that I had ventured into the mysteries of cooking. I was suffering from the novice's blind enthusiasm for meager accomplishment. I'm sure that if Houdini had a daughter, she at least once insisted that he watch her untie her shoes.

But I still want to know what went wrong with my calculations. Candy is the one with no earthly notion of what one number has to do with another, and what either has to do with anything in this world. Once when she was trying to figure out her age, I told her, "Well, you were born in 1948, and it's 1977 now," and she looked at me indignantly and said, "So?" But I was always pretty good at math, back when it was comprehensible, and I was the one who tripled the recipe that had been plenty for just the two of us. Anyone would think that three times enough for two hearty eaters would be plenty for us and Murray and Nancy and the other couple we'd invited. Three times two *is* six, isn't it?

There was the problem, too, of presentation. Nowadays, if I were to serve cannelloni as a main course with just a salad, I wouldn't put the salad off in separate bowls and I wouldn't use large dinner plates on which to dish out two rolls of cannelloni as if they were a full serving. Candy and I looked at each other in dismay.

I have never seen cannelloni disappear so fast. I was subjected several times, when I was a boy, to a particular preacher's story about some hound dogs who, when their owner threw out the leftovers after every meal, would catch them in the air. One day, the preacher said, what was left over was boiled okra, which everybody in Mississippi then knew was *slick*, and when the hounds caught it, it slid down their throats so fast that they stood there puzzled for a minute and then started sniffing the ground. I never thought much of the joke, or of the preacher for that matter, but our guests looked just the way those hounds must have.

After that evening of humiliation and hunger, I was ready to take Stephen Leacock's advice: "If at first you don't succeed, quit, quit at once." But our new, untried kitchen soon had me hanging around it, making tentative forays toward its working parts. Candy prodded me a little, too. Her meals, when she lived alone, seem to have consisted of an occasional steak grilled on her hibachi, a potato now and then, and sometimes some macaroni and cheese, the only thing out of a box I've ever known her to tolerate. She was ready for a good full dinner every evening and for variations of our menu that local restaurants didn't provide to the satisfaction of either of us.

The biggest single boost to my interest in cooking was, in fact, the wok Candy gave me for Christmas when she judged the time was right. It was. Her mother called her aside and said, "Couldn't you have given him something a little more personal?" But she couldn't have, and, knowing that, I knew I was in for a long relationship with the cookstove.

STEAK and POTATOES

I think that the way we broiled steaks when we started out was to sprinkle them with salt and pepper and slap them on the little hibachi. Over the years that has evolved toward what is sometimes called the Florentine manner. Our favorites are porterhouse, Delmonico, or rib eye steaks cut at least an inch thick; blot them dry with paper towels, grind on a fair amount of black pepper, and rub them with olive oil. Have the coals good and hot, so that they sear the steaks rather quickly. When the down sides have a nice color, turn the steaks and let the other sides catch up. (Be ready to move the steaks aside for a spell while flames lap up the melted fat.) Squeeze on lemon juice and attack with knife and fork.

As for potatoes, scrub clean a couple of large Idahos, wipe them dry with a paper towel, and then either wrap them in foil (if you want them steamed), or rub them with olive oil, or leave them dry (if you like the skin crisp). Stick them in a 350-degree oven for about an hour, until they just squeeze good. We like them without all the sour cream and gunk people started putting on them a while back—just butter, a little salt, and a pleasant sprinkling of freshly ground pepper.

CANNELLONI

I think I have blotted out all memory of that early cannelloni recipe, except that I did wrap the filling in raw pasta, and the filling did involve ricotta and spinach and probably ground meat. In any case, I still make cannelloni, at least for just us, but I have no set recipe. The sauce varies according to whether fresh tomatoes are in season, what herbs are available, and the whim of the moment. Sometimes I put in a middle layer; sometimes I include some of its ingredients in the sauce and use that both between layers and on top; sometimes I put in bacon, and sometimes I don't; the mozzarella is optional, too. Anyway, here's a sort of basic recipe from which to leave out things:

FILLING

1 pound ground chuck, sautéed in 1 tablespoon olive oil, drained, with a little salt and a couple of grinds of black pepper
1 pound fresh raw spinach, or 10-ounce package frozen
A couple of grates of nutmeg
1 pound ricotta
4 slices crisply fried bacon, crumbled

PASTA

4 eggs' worth of pasta, rolled thin and cut into squares 4 inches or so across (see pasta recipe, p. 87)

MIDLAYER
Sauté until soft

> *1 medium onion, chopped*
> *2 medium bell peppers, chopped*
> *1 large carrot, chopped*

in

> *1 tablespoon olive oil*

Add, and cook another minute or two

> *1 tablespoon chopped fresh herbs, or 1/2 teaspoon dried oregano*
> *A pinch of salt*
> *A couple of grinds of black pepper*
> *A pinch of red pepper flakes*

SAUCE
Cook down until fairly thick

> *4 large ripe tomatoes, peeled, seeded, and chopped, or 1 small can (16 ounces) Italian plum tomatoes*
> *1 large clove garlic, minced*
> *1 tablespoon chopped fresh basil, or 1 teaspoon dried*
> *1 tablespoon chopped fresh oregano, or 1/2 teaspoon dried*
> *1 tablespoon chopped fresh parsley, Italian if available*
> *A pinch of salt*
> *A couple of grinds of black pepper*
> *1/4 teaspoon red pepper flakes*

TOPPING

> *1/2 pound mozzarella, sliced*

The fresh spinach should be washed (but not dried), stemmed, and put over low heat in a covered pot until wilted, then drained and chopped. For frozen spinach, put the chunk in a pot over low heat, cover, pull apart with a fork as it thaws; let it warm through, then drain and chop. Grate the nutmeg over the chopped spinach. When no one is looking, drink the pot liquor.

Mix the ground chuck, chopped spinach, ricotta, and bacon thoroughly. Roll it in the pasta squares, which either are left raw or have been cooked in boiling water until they swell a bit (I do it one way sometimes, sometimes the other). Layer the ingredients in a casserole dish lightly coated with olive oil, in this order: half the filled pasta, onion-pepper-carrot midlayer, remaining filled pasta, most of the sauce, mozzarella topping, and enough reserved sauce to give it color. Bake at 350 degrees for half an hour or a little more. This should make enough for at least four people, but if I were you I wouldn't trust me on that score.

PIZZA

Our favorite pizza now is much simpler than the pizza I originally concocted. For one thing, in the summer months the sauce is just fresh tomatoes—peeled, seeded, squeezed as dry as possible, and chopped. That's all. Not even salt or pepper. Canned Italian plum tomatoes will do in winter, or, better, the fresh plum tomatoes from Yarnell's Farm Market up the road that I peeled and froze a couple of years ago (about half of them pureed in the Cuisinart, so that the whole ones were immersed in liquid). But mostly we just wait till tomatoes are ripe on the vines in Candy's garden plot.

The toppings are less complex, too, although I now start with either mozzarella or provolone, in slices cut as thin as possible and overlapped to seal the crust. This keeps the juices from making it soggy. On the coating of cheese I spread a little chopped tomato. Then on one pizza (this recipe makes two, both rather rich) I put sautéed ground chuck and black olives covered with additional slices of cheese. On the other we like thinly sliced pepperoni and sliced fresh mushrooms, plus the additional cheese. Lately I have been using provolone for both the bottom and top layers, but sometimes I use mozzarella for one and provolone for the other. The proportions run something like this:

TOPPING

- 1 ½ *pounds mozzarella or provolone, thinly sliced*
- 2 *very large tomatoes or the equivalent, peeled, seeded, squeezed dry, and chopped*
- 1 *pound ground chuck, sautéed in 1 tablespoon olive oil, drained, with a little salt and freshly ground black pepper*

1 can small, whole California black olives, drained
3 or 4 ounces pepperoni, thinly sliced
½ pound fresh mushrooms, sliced

Obviously, infinite variations are possible, but the one thing not to vary is the crust. I have no way of tracing where the recipe came from; I think it may have shown up in a newspaper. In any case, the idea is to roll the dough out as thin as possible (work from the middle outward; this takes patience), perforate it and prebake it. It yields enough thin crust for the two pizzas, enough to feed four people.

PIZZA CRUST

1 ½ cups unbleached flour
1 ½ tablespoons olive oil
½ cup tepid water
½ teaspoon dry yeast
½ teaspoon salt

Mix, knead, roll out thin, perforate with the tines of a fork, and prebake at 350 degrees until it begins to look brown. Top the crust as indicated above and cook in a 450-degree oven until cheese is bubbling and beginning to brown. Remove immediately to rack to keep the crust from becoming soggy.

SPICY PIZZA

The following recipe is one that I contributed to *A Man's Taste* some years ago, refined a little. It is close to my original spicy pizza but really features cheeses. Or so I thought; the editorial note with the recipe said, "This is the best crust I have ever tasted." Anyway, here's what goes on top of the crust:

CHEESES

5 parts mozzarella
2 parts Monterey Jack

2 parts baby Swiss
1 part sharp cheddar

SAUCE

In

1 tablespoon olive oil

Sauté

1 small onion, minced
1 small bell pepper, minced

Add, and simmer a few minutes

8 ounces plum tomatoes, pureed
1 clove garlic, pressed
1 tablespoon parsley, minced
½ teaspoon dried tarragon
½ teaspoon dried thyme
½ teaspoon dried oregano
A large pinch each of cayenne, black pepper, ground sage, and cumin

TOPPINGS

½ pound ground chuck, sautéed in ½ tablespoon olive oil, drained, with a little salt and pepper
½ can black olives, drained and halved
½ pound fresh mushrooms, sliced

Cover prebaked crust with overlapping very thin slices of mozzarella, then add sauce, meat and olive toppings, and additional cheeses (shredded or thinly sliced, so that however cheesy you like your pizza you end up with the proportions noted). Bake in a 450-degree oven, lower part, until cheeses are bubbling and beginning to brown. Remove. Add mushrooms, and return pizzas to oven until they're heated through. Remove immediately to rack.

 The chief refinement in the spicy pizza recipe, other than sealing off the crust with cheese slices, is that I originally used canned tomato sauce. But since now, perhaps snobbishly, I tend to put down cookbooks as soon as I see "1 large can tomato sauce" or "1 can mushroom soup," I have substituted the plum tomatoes. I don't think it's really snobbish. Canned soups in general seem to be largely intensified salt in liquid form, and canned tomato sauces have an acidic, tinny taste.

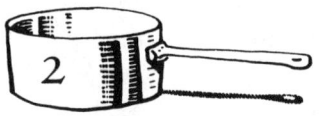

Escoffier, Je Suis Ici

If you disagreed with one of my old professors long enough, he would concede that "it all comes down to a matter of taste, finally." Then he would add, "And I think mine is very good." He was talking about literary taste, of course, and he had at least some reason to think that his was good. Once when I kept offering a reading of a Ben Jonson poem different from his, he ended the conversation with, "Have you read the entire works of Jonson? Well, I have."

Taste is acquired, I grant. We're not likely to recognize the best in poetry or art or music or cuisine without having read or looked at or heard or eaten some of the best. And most often we have to learn from somebody or some tradition before we know what to taste for. Let experts train and prune as they will, however, individual taste grows out of the same tangle as does individual temperament.

Part of that tangle has to do with the flavors and textures shoveled across our tongues in our formative years. A while back, when my friend Louie and I were judges at a chili cookoff, another judge exclaimed over a particular entry, "Say! That's good!" Louie and I looked at each other in alarm. The concoction had seemed to us nothing but limp spaghetti and canned tomato soup. After a minute, our fellow judge said, "It's just the way my mother used to make it."

I still love what my mother made, and what she cooks now. Old Southern home cooking, as practiced by my grandmother and the mothers of some of my friends, along with my mother's variations and additions, constituted for me what cooking was. Infrequent visits with my Sicilian father's side of the family gave me an idea of an exotic and varied other world, but I was only ten at the last of those visits—until reestablishing contact in my middle age—and instead of setting my standards by the dishes served up by my Uncle George's chef, I lapsed into the generality that Italian food is good stuff.

I tried it in restaurants; mostly what I got was spaghetti, of course, under a very acid tomato sauce heavy with oregano and garlic, topped with meatballs. I have never really liked meatballs, and that sauce was like nothing I tasted in Italy, when I finally got over there. Most Americanized Italian fare reminds me of a recent TV commercial: Some people at a Japanese restaurant are about to take off their shoes; one man stops short and thinks, "Foot odor!" Then he says, "Uh, let's eat Italian."

I enjoy good Italian food, and I cook it, or my version of some of its dishes, as often as any other. Of course, the wok Candy gave me opened up stir-fry for us. I had been partial to Chinese food since my first visit to San Francisco's Chinatown during World War II. I can still see the upstairs restaurant, the bud vase on the table, the friend in sailor blues sitting across from me, as my first bite of tempura shrimp imprinted the scene in my head. This is the place, I probably would have said if I had been Brigham Young; years passed before I discovered that tempura was Japanese.

I've never had shrimp as astonishingly good anywhere since, and probably never will, but I have eaten some very enjoyable Chinese meals in restaurants in and around San Francisco, in New York's Chinatown, and even in Columbus, Ohio. But just as you can tell a dish is Italian by the sharp tomatoes and garlic and oregano, in most places you can tell it's Chinese because it's goopy with cornstarch and masked out with soy sauce and MSG. I suppose that's the way its sameness of flavor is achieved, sort of like going heavy with the grease so people will know it's Southern.

One of my Mississippi uncles used to tell about climbing into the attic of a country church and waiting till the spirit was really moving the congregation, and one woman was carrying on, saying, "I see Jesus! I see Jesus!" According to his story, he lowered a jack-o'-lantern right in front of her face, and she stopped and said, "I do see *something*." I've had her kind of experience in more Southern, Italian, and Chinese restaurants than I care to think about. And Mexican. And even French.

The French have always had close ties with us Americans—Lafayette even came over and helped fight our Revolution, and General Pershing took our troops over there in 1917 to immortalize the line "Lafayette, we are here." But I'm not sure why I singled out French cuisine as the best, or potentially the best. I've known all along that it's thought of that way by batches of people, but I usually resist conformity, or find out later that I've been swept along a step and a half behind without having observed that I was doing what everybody else was already getting bored with. Julia Child had something to do with my fixation upon French, coming onto television about the time I became interested in cooking. So did a dinner (even though of the eating all I remember is dipping fresh vegetables into hot oil flavored with fresh garlic) in a restaurant clinging to a hillside near Grasse, with giant copper pots hanging against the stone of the huge fireplace.

And so did the bread in France. I don't think I found the food there better than that in Italy, but there was a distinct difference in the bread as soon as you crossed the border. Now you can get good French bread over here—good, but not as light and magical as it was there. I have learned to prefer the somewhat heavier Italian bread with many dishes, but eating bread for the first time in France was like having the sun come out, or biting into that first tempura shrimp.

Where, though, did I come up with Escoffier as my ideal? I don't even know how I came to hear about him. Maybe the name was born into me in some way, and as soon as I heard it I knew. Maybe French cuisine is in my genes, or something. It could possibly have come through my father, since the French as well as the Phoenicians, the Saracens, the Normans, the Greeks, the Romans, the Spanish, the Austrians, the English, and the Americans have taken over Sicily at one time or another, although I have no reason to believe that the French got more blood into my line than any of the others—except the Americans, of course, who arrived too late to affect me.

My Mississippi grandmother, one of the most opinionated people who ever lived, is supposed to have been visited in her eighties by some Texans who had looked into the genealogy of the Matheny clan, of which she was a member. "Yes," my grandmother told them, "we're all Scotch-Irish." "No, no," they said, "You're French." My grandmother sat for a moment before she said, "And I've never liked the French."

Maybe that's all true. I've certainly never liked the French more than other people, although I found them friendly and helpful when I was in their country. But the country itself, or at least part of it, seemed like my place. It was north of the Pyrenees as we drove toward Toulouse. I have no idea why, but going through that green and pleasant land, with the road gently curving through fields and trees, I kept feeling as though I were on the verge of recognizing the place, as if around the next turn, there I'd be: home.

It didn't happen. But maybe Escoffier has something to do with all this. I don't know. All I know is that someday I hope to do a French dish so well that I can say, "Escoffier, *je suis ici*." He doesn't have to answer. I don't think Lafayette said anything back to General Pershing. But, of course, Pershing didn't even *try* to speak in French.

FRENCH BREAD

A few years ago Julia Child and her husband worked out a way to make French bread that comes about as close to that in France as we can in this country. I fiddled around with their method—lots of risings, tiles and a pan of hot water in the oven, and what not—but that was before I had any idea what I was doing, so I have never been able to judge whether it's worth all the trouble. Eventually, I just took the basic ingredients for French bread, worked out my own proportions, and began to do it my way, which would incite a French baker to murder and get him acquitted in any fair trial.

I make four loaves at a time and freeze them, so that we can cut off a third of a loaf and heat it up to have with a pasta dish we've decided on at the last moment, or stick a loaf or two in a low oven half an hour before calling company to the table.

One of my large stainless-steel bowls weighs ¾ pound; I put it on the scales, set them for 2¾ pounds, and scoop in flour till they let me know I have

2 pounds unbleached flour

Two pounds should equal about 7 cups, but weighing is easier and a little more accurate, or so I'm told, although it doesn't prevent variations in the resulting dough. Mix into the flour

3 teaspoons salt
2 packages dry yeast

Stir in slowly

3 cups warm water (not over 130 degrees)

Mix thoroughly, then knead for about 10 minutes. (If you use a mixer with dough hooks, stir the flour mixture into the water on low speed for 45 seconds, then knead on medium speed for 8 minutes.) Add a little flour if necessary; the dough should be somewhat tacky but elastic. Scrape it out into a large oiled bowl (I use one of glazed earthenware), roll it around until it's oiled all over, and let it rise until it has doubled in volume. It should rise in a warm, draft-free place, so I cheat and put it in the oven, preheated to the lowest setting and turned off. A sheet of wax paper laid over the bowl helps keep the dough from drying too much on top.

After an hour or an hour and a half, when the dough appears to have doubled, dump it out onto a floured board—using floured hands to detach it from the bowl—and knead briefly, adding flour as necessary; the idea is to keep it from being tacky and to give it enough body and elasticity to form loaves that can rise upward rather than spread out in glutenless apathy. Divide the dough into fourths with a scraper, press out each fourth into a flat oval, fold over and then over again to make a long loaf, shape it gently, and put it onto a pan sprinkled generously with

Cornmeal

I use a 16 × 16-inch heavy black cookie sheet, which holds the four loaves perfectly—well, holds them perfectly if I concoct them perfectly.

The loaves go into the oven, which is still somewhat warm, on the bottom rack, with sheets of wax paper on the rack immediately above, to rise until they have doubled in size again. Then remove them from the oven, set a rack in the top third of the oven, and preheat to 425 degrees. Cut three diagonal scars into the top of each loaf with a sharp knife or razor, holding it almost parallel with the surface. If the dough is at all tacky, this can be a mess. I haven't found a cutting implement that really works; I gave up on razor blades long ago; now with the serrated knife that is usually assigned the task of cutting lemons or limes, I try to slice in, often sort of dragging the surface along, and let it do. My daughter, Nina, uses scissors and cuts into the loaves before they rise. I may give that a try; she's a better baker than I am.

Put the pan of mangled loaves into the oven on the top rack. After about 15 minutes, take a peek. When the loaves are coloring up nicely, remove them from the oven, take them off the pan (I usually have to separate them from each other with a knife or metal spatula), and return them to the oven, directly on the rack, for another 5 minutes or so, until the bottoms have browned a bit and sound hollow when you thump them—the way we used to thump watermelons when I was a boy to see if they were ripe. Let them cool on a rack.

The loaves aren't glazed, and the crust is not light and crisp but rather thickish and a bit chewy. You'd think we lazy and inept cooks should dare to feed only the ignorant, but even our gourmet friends join us in liking the color and texture and flavor of this bread. We have had so many guests gobble it up, brag on it, ask for more, and even request it in advance of being asked to dinner, that I have pretty much stuck with it.

It's nearer to Italian than French, really, but if your guests are sophisticated, it might be wise to leave off any national designation rather than invite comparisons.

II

The Meeting

"Gertrude raised her head and directed towards the young nobleman two eyes so eyelike in their expression as to be absolutely circular, while Lord Ronald directed towards the occupant of the dogcart a gaze so gazelike that nothing but a gazelle or a gas-pipe could have emulated its intensity."

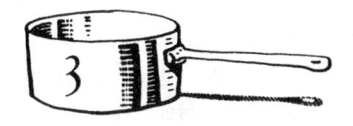

La Cuisine, C'est Moi

Before I fell into the habit myself, it used to irritate me when women friends would chatter away about "our house," "our bedroom," "our broom closet," and "*my* kitchen."

I'd want to whisper to Candy, "How often do you suppose she picks up *her* toys and goes home to mother?" I was in no danger with Candy; she might claim the couch, or three-quarters of it, but she'd never say "my kitchen."

"*My* kitchen," I would think indignantly. "Indeed!"

Why it mattered to me, I now suspect, was that, however smugly I might refer to our kitchen as ours, it had never granted either of us property rights.

For a good while it belonged more to our friend Irene than to anybody else. When she would come for a visit, she'd sweep fearlessly in, relocate the pots and pans, alphabetize the spice shelf, and whomp us up a good batch of beef Stroganoff. We'd hang back, pretending to help, and beg her *please* to stay and be our mother.

The way Irene manhandled recipes as well as the kitchen put me in awe. "Have you no respect for the printed word?" something in me wanted to demand, all the time my mouth was watering in anticipation of whatever she was audaciously concocting. I was like a kid who is shocked that a daring friend will crawl through a fence and steal a watermelon off the vine, but can't wait to gouge out his share of the heart.

Beef Stroganoff Irene, as I have it labeled in my card file, was wrenched out of a recipe from the first cookbook Candy and I owned. It may seem elementary now, but I was appalled when Irene substituted white wine for "¼ cup sherry or red wine," added an uncalled-for minced clove of garlic and a dash each of Tabasco and Worcestershire sauce, then, with utter disregard for the sanctity of the page, wrote in heavy pencil beside instructions to serve with wild or brown rice, "Use noodles. LARGE PKG." and, down below, "Put parsley, butter, Parmesan in noodles," and "Rewarms good!"

Gaining sustenance was exciting when Irene was here, but what Candy and I ate on our own before I took over the kitchen is nearly as much a blank as, according to some accounts, their pre-human-language feral existence is to children raised by wolves. I suspect that, except for a few feeble attempts at something different, we had merely regularized Candy's efficiency apartment diet. If we had had our own dump for archaeologists to muck about in off in the dim dark future, they'd probably turn up nothing but steak bones, along with little wads of aluminum foil that had once been wrapped, as Shroud of Turin scientists would have no difficulty establishing, around potatoes.

Our choice of food was dictated in part by Candy's way of fastening upon things. What would she like to eat tonight? "Steaks." What *would* she eat if no good steaks were available? "Nothing." She'd go through a market the same way I've seen her barge through a clothing store, dismissing without pause everything within and beyond her peripheral vision, until suddenly she veers off toward a wool sweater, or a cowboy hat, or slippers shaped like hippo feet. Once she's fixed on whatever it is, you could stack up within what you think is her range of vision all the riches of the Indies and never excite a movement of the eyeballs.

Eventually we were forced to recognize that kitchens as well as Candy took an active interest in limiting our diet. As long as we were really cooking outside on the grill, we seemed allowed our two potatoes in the oven, but just let us start to shift the balance indoors and whatever kitchen shared our living space would turn on us what is called in Italian its *batteria di cucina*.

Candy gave it the initial try. She decided on béarnaise sauce to fancy up our steaks the very first time our friends Maurie and JoAnn had the misfortune of dining with us. Believe me, it is worse than a slap on the wrist to have perfectly good wine and shallots and tarragon combine with egg yolks and butter to make your mouth feel as though it has been sucking burnt pennies. Maurie, tough from the day he was born, was the only one who could even make a show of eating it. After that béarnaise, Maurie always stuffed his pockets with

Gelusil tablets before coming to dinner at our house; none of us realized how desperately he would need them as I began my skirmishes with the kitchen.

I'm not sure just what all lured me into combat, though I do think now that I should have gone about it more boldly. I've wondered since why I didn't learn something from watching Irene. But then, roomfuls of people don't lapse from their small talk upon my entrance, much less focus upon me as though waiting for the Word of the Day, the way they do Irene; to expect the response she got from the kitchen would have been like walking into a cage of big cats with the cockeyed assurance that they'd roll over and play dead. If I had fancied myself as blessed as Daniel or as skilled as Gunther Gebel-Williams, I might have gone the way of who knows how many would-be circus performers in unmarked graves near Sarasota, Florida.

Still, I do think I should have gone about it with more confidence than I did. Part of it wasn't so much fear of the kitchen, real as that was, as a simple misunderstanding: I had the effect confused with the effort. When I tried a delicate crabmeat appetizer with hollandaise, I went *at* it delicately; I should have remembered the incredible strength apparent in Arthur Rubinstein's hands as he played even the most airy Chopin étude. I should have remembered, too, hearing a man named Steinway say on public radio that Rubinstein had his piano tuned to just *his* sound and the action set to fit *his* attack, so he and Vladimir Horowitz couldn't have performed well on each other's piano if they had wanted to. In short, I should have known, I suppose, that I had to make the kitchen *mine*; I had to master it with force and use it with assurance before I could produce the subtle reverberations of, for instance, an Escoffier-inspired sauce.

The time I went at the hollandaise with delicacy instead of strength requires a full account later, possibly before a grand jury. Not only was it the nadir of Maurie and JoAnn's culinary experience with us, but it left me convinced that my idol Julia Child and her cohorts in volume one of *Mastering the Art of French Cooking* had lied to me when they spoke of "five minutes." In my hands at that stage, of course, the "Minute Waltz" would have become the "All-Evening Hesitation"; it took me a long, long time to discover that Julia knew what she was talking about.

Meanwhile I had fought doggedly through defeat and, inch by grudging inch, occupied the kitchen. I think my first victory was in deliberately unalphabetizing the spice cabinet: Irene could work that way, but for the fifty or so weeks of the year that she wasn't around, I was fumbling into the most inaccessible spaces for the most used herbs. It wasn't easy to put the thyme up front and move the cardomom to the rear—Irene is, after all, one of my favorite people in the world—but there are, in *l'amour, la guerre,* and *la cuisine,* higher considerations than friendship.

I quit being intimidated by appliances, too. After scraping burnt stuff out of saucepan bottoms for a couple of years, I realized that the words printed on my stove top didn't have sufficient authority to overrule the actual relationship of flame to food. " 'Simmer,' you say?" I learned to respond. "Don't tell me 'simmer.' I'll know simmer when I by God see it." In fact, I had to lower the control to "warm" and put on one of those flame-tamers to get my beef bourguignon cauldron down to its proper bubble.

I even had a mercenary come in and help do the kitchen over to suit me. Tore out a wall and took in the entryway for more room. Cut an opening to the living area so people waiting to eat could look in and see that I hadn't gone to sleep. Moved the spice cabinet—lock, stock, and basil—clear across the room. Added a convection oven. Hung pots from beams and swung a utensil hanger above the sink. In short, although my overall attack was more a siege than a *coup de cuisine,* I took the damn thing over.

But I was, with considerable assurance, doing mayonnaise, béarnaise, and even suprêmes de volaille à la bordelaise before I began to work with hollandaise again. Eventually I managed to get the time down to half an hour, but I still considered it my bête noire; I'm certain that, like any beast, it could smell fear no matter how nonchalant I tried to appear. Until the other night. You've put oil into egg yolks before, I told myself. Butter is no different.

It turned out not to be. "I want you to be a witness," I said to Candy through my opening in the wall. "I have just done a hollandaise in five minutes." She was, as usual, stretched out on the couch, propped against the pillows on the far end, absorbed in a book. "It's just perfect, too." I gave it one last whisk, turned off the heat, lifted the heavy porcelain double boiler away from the hot water beneath, and cried, "Voila!" just as it began to curdle.

Candy looked up. "Did you say something?"

"Forget it. I'm just trying to remember . . . something about cold water."

A while back I would have been paralyzed: Does cold water mean ice water, refrigerator water, or water from the tap marked "cold"? How much? And should it be dumped in all at once? Poured in a stream? Added by drops?

Not now. I reached into the refrigerator, grabbed a bottle of Perrier, splashed a little into the curdling hollandaise, whisked briskly a time or two, and there *was* a perfect hollandaise, in only five minutes—and, well, twenty or thirty seconds. Julia Child, *je suis arrivé*.

BEEF STROGANOFF IRENE

The recipe that Irene took over belongs, in its original state, to a Mrs. Wallace Johnston. I'm sure it's delicious as Mrs. Johnston wrote it up, but I've never had it that way, and I do love it with Irene's alterations. Either way it calls for 1 ½ pounds beef tenderloin, which is said to serve six; the last time I made it, I used a bit more than that, and it just did for three of us—although some noodles and sauce were left over. That may well be because I cooked the tenderloin whole and sliced it, an alternative the original recipe suggests, so that the noodles were served on the side and the sauce was napped onto the meat. When the meat is cut into "thin strips two inches long" and sautéed in butter, as the recipe proper directs, and especially if it is all ladled over wild or brown rice, or noodles, eaters are encouraged to focus less on the tenderloin and take in more of the accompaniments—but, still, I'd allow a half-pound of tenderloin per any person I've observed dine at my table, except for our back-fence neighbor, Marge, who weighs nothing and eats less. So, here's about what I'd do for four people:

THE BEEF
Sauté

2 pounds beef tenderloin, cut into thin 2-inch strips

in

3 tablespoons butter

for a minute; spoon onto a hot platter; dish on sauce (below), and serve, as I've said, with wild or brown rice, or with a couple of eggs' worth of noodles (see p. 87), which may be enriched with chopped parsley, butter, and freshly grated Parmigiano.

To cook the tenderloin whole, I use a method learned from a recipe in *Gourmet* magazine: If the tenderloin is not the same thickness throughout, fold the tail back and pin it with toothpicks to correct that situation as nearly as possible. Rub the tenderloin, at room temperature, with vegetable oil, sprinkle it with a little salt and a few grinds of black pepper, put it in a pan and cook it for twenty-three minutes in a 550-degree oven. Take it out and let it sit for fifteen minutes more, loosely covered with aluminum foil. Then slice it rather thin—¼ to ½ inch thick. Arrange on a hot platter, nap with the sauce, and serve the remaining sauce alongside.

THE SAUCE

1 onion, chopped
1 tablespoon butter
¾ to 1 pound mushrooms, sliced
¼ cup red or white wine
2 cups sour cream
½ teaspoon salt
Several grinds of black pepper
A couple of dashes of Tabasco
A couple of dashes of Worcestershire sauce
The juices from slicing the tenderloin, if cooked whole

Sauté the onion in the butter until soft, add the mushrooms, and stir for a minute; pour in the wine and cook until almost dry. Add the sour cream, salt, pepper, Tabasco, Worcestershire sauce, and juices, and heat through carefully. If sour cream is heated too long it loses body, and the sauce should be thick.

Serve it up: A loaf of bread, a jug of wine—ah, Stroganoff were paradise enow! But throw in a green salad for good measure.

BEEF BOURGUIGNON

Or boeuf bourguignon. Or boeuf bourguignonne. Whatever. The stuff I have to cook over a flame tamer to keep from gumming up the bottom of the pot is one of my early recipes, adapted from a recipe one page ahead of the one for Stroganoff Irene marked up in the Memphis *Woman's Exchange Cookbook*. With Irene's example, I mustered courage enough to change Mrs. Henry R. Lake's recipe, and I even took a *pen* to it—not an erasable pencil the way Irene did. I marked out "1 lg. can mushrooms" as boldly as I dared; I don't, and didn't then, use canned mushrooms, what with fresh ones so abundant on produce shelves, but the fresh ones I tried in the recipe detracted from the flavor, it seemed to Candy and me. I also marked out "2 bay leaves, crushed" and printed beside it "TARRAGON," because the bay leaves on hand then were some of the domestic ones that have, for us, an odd taste.

What I didn't mark, but changed nevertheless, was "1 can beef consommé." When I first tried the recipe with no consommé on hand, I dissolved a couple of beef bouillon cubes in 2 cups of hot water and whisked what seemed like enough of that (about 10 ounces) into the roux that thickens the pot. Now I generally use one bouillon cube and a couple of tablespoons of the meat glaze that most of the stock I make gets simmered down to (see p. 171). I also changed "1 teaspoon salt" to "½ teaspoon salt," but since that adjustment was made I have gone in fact to no salt at all. The bouillon cube is salty enough, along with the bacon.

So now the recipe goes pretty much like this:

BEEF BOURGUIGNON

6 slices bacon, cut into small pieces
4 pounds sirloin, trimmed and cut into strips "size of medium french fries," as Mrs. Lake aptly puts it
2 garlic cloves, minced
6 green onions, minced
2 tablespoons chopped parsley
1 teaspoon dried tarragon
1 imported bay leaf
1 teaspoon dried thyme
Several grinds of black pepper
½ cup butter
½ cup flour
1 beef bouillon cube and 2 tablespoons meat glaze in 10 ounces boiling water (or 2 bouillon cubes in 16 ounces boiling water; use 10 ounces in the recipe and drink the rest)
12 ounces dry red wine
2 tablespoons fresh lemon juice

Fry the bacon in a large heavy pot and remove. Sauté the sirloin strips in the bacon grease, add the garlic, green onions, parsley, tarragon, bay leaf, thyme, black pepper, and the fried bits of bacon. Melt the butter in a saucepan over low heat and stir in the flour until well combined; after a moment, whisk in the bouillon–meat glaze mixture, then the wine, and then the lemon juice. Cook until thickened, then add to the pot, mixing well. Cover and simmer for a couple of hours. (Don't forget to remove the bay leaf.)

The recipe will serve six people on a cold winter night, but it's great for just the two of us, because warmed over it's possibly even better than when it's first cooked. Since that's the case, it can be made well in advance, refrigerated or frozen, and then allowed to heat to a slow bubble in time for company to sit down at the table.

We like it with freshly made noodles or with rice (either on the side or with the beef bourguignon spooned on top), a loaf of French bread split, buttered, and heated in a 300-degree oven until it begins to toast (about twenty-five minutes), a salad of crisp lettuce or spinach, and a bottle of red wine hearty enough to hold its own. Makes me hungry to think about it.

HOLLANDAISE SAUCE

I have over a period of time made hollandaise by various recipes and with varying degrees of success, ranging from complete separation to runniness to near perfection. The first recipe that really seems to suit me, though, both in my feeling secure with it and in the quality of the results, is one that my daughter-in-law, Becky, learned from her mother, Edith, and taught to me. It works, and it produces a smooth, tasty sauce that has full body without being stiff.

EDITH'S HOLLANDAISE SAUCE

Use a double boiler, and start with the water cold. Don't let the water touch the bottom of the top boiler, and don't let it ever come to a boil. Use a wooden spoon, not a whisk, throughout the cooking.

On the stove, put into the cold double boiler

2 egg yolks, beaten
1 tablespoon fresh lemon juice
A pinch of salt
$1/3$ stick unsalted butter, cold; hold additional $2/3$ stick

Turn heat on, low, and stir ingredients slowly until the butter melts; if the egg mixture begins to thicken too much around the edges, raise the boiler from the hot water for a moment (and check, too, to be sure that the water isn't boiling); add the second third of butter and repeat; add the third portion of butter and repeat; when all the butter is melted, whip the sauce a couple of strokes with the wooden spoon. Use immediately.

By the Book

I am a real sucker for cookbooks, and I keep adding to my collection even though within the twelve linear feet I've provided for them there really isn't space for more. One little set, a dozen inches wide, faces into the dining area so that eaters may gain confidence from the spines of *The New Larousse Gastronomique*, the *Gourmet Cookbook* in two volumes, boxed, that Irene gave us, and a couple of translations of Escoffier. But most of them are on the shelves I put up in the kitchen after we took in the entryway, including what I finally added over the front door. The only shelf brackets that would fit into that space were more flexible than they should have been, and for a while the books would gradually work loose and threaten to avalanche upon some unsuspecting guest. But since the people I'd like to see buried under hardbacks never darken our doorway, I fixed the shelf to the overhead beams with metal rods.

Every new book means a new decision: whether to banish a volume that seldom gets looked into, or take down one of the copper pots we set up to frame the books and serve as reminders that the abstractions within their covers are meant to have physical consequences. Books have already displaced all of the pots but two: a small oval casserole and the low heavy potatoes-Anna pan, with its overhanging top and double set of flat ears. For nearly three months now, M. F. K. Fisher's *The Art of Eating* has been taking up precious counter space while I have been unable to find a book that thick I want to take down and unwilling to hide one of the pots in a cabinet. Mustn't rush into anything, I always say.

When I do open a place, it's not a matter of just sticking the new book into the old slot. General cookbooks have their own territory; the rest are flocked together mostly by section or nation or hemisphere. The space between the refrigerator and the utility-room door, for instance, just exactly holds all the Oriental and Italian cookbooks—strange shelf-fellows, perhaps, but that's where they fit, and there does seem to have been some sort of pasta/noodle exchange between the two cuisines as far back as Marco Polo. One more volume of Szechuan or Tuscan recipes, though, will set off an intercontinental game of fruit-basket turnover.

Magazines are even harder to deal with, not to mention clippings and pamphlets. The latter have been tossed onto a silver chest (i.e., a case for stainless flatware) in a low cabinet; behind them, accessible from the dining room, is a double stack of magazines, through which I usually search in vain for the one listed on a card in my recipe file before I discover that it's in the separate stack shelved beneath the top of the mobile cutting board. Irene is ordering cases for the magazines, however, and one of these days there will be organization—probably when she comes to visit and sees to it.

Keeping the printed matter in some sort of order is enough of a problem, but things get worse when you try to cook from it. For a long time I kept a big Plexiglas holder between the pasta machine fastened at the end of a counter and the television set backed up in the corner. It was apparent all along that it took up a lot of space, but I didn't realize how much trouble it was—such a simple device, after all, with no moving parts—until it had sat there unused for what must have been months, staring vacantly at nothing through a glaze of reflected light.

Reflection had been one of the problems: To keep the glare from shutting out the recipe I was trying to follow, the holder had to be angled toward the front wall, and I had to press up against the front counter, twisted into a position that the Discus Thrower has sustained gracefully for centuries but that put cramps in my neck and back within seconds.

Even so, the holder might not have been exiled to the garage if every recipe in every book were complete on one page or on two pages that open out together. When a recipe wasn't, I'd always clunk the book against the overhead cabinet a couple of times before I could get the holder out from under; then I'd have to lift the book and try to turn the page with a dripping whisk or wooden spoon in hand, fit the book back in carefully so as not to wad or tear, slide the holder under the cabinet again, position it for the light, torque myself into reading position, and realize that I no longer remembered what led into "———ing carefully as you do so" at the top of the new page.

Although it's what I've come to again, laying the books out doesn't solve that problem. Most cookbooks won't stay open at the right place without being weighted by something as heavy as the half-filled kettle or the greasy bacon press. I no longer mind very much the spatters and half-moons of oil, batter, and general gunk that decorate their pages; the problem is that when you nudge the kettle far enough off to read the recipe, as well as when you lift it off to turn the page, the book folds up in your face.

The only suitable places to lay open the books, in my kitchen, are the cutting boards and the marble slab, all of which I need for work space. I have put books on top of the convection oven and on a gas burner—when they're not on, of course; the dish drain in the far sink might work if I didn't keep the rolling cutting board in front of it when the regular oven is in use. Really, what I need is a sort of music-stand device mounted on the front of a menial whose job would be to follow me around, staying carefully out of the way, and turn pages—forward, and then back again so I can reread that forgotten beginning of a sentence—at a nod.

Either that or demand that all cookbooks be set up, like those of Pierre Franey, so that pages don't have to be turned. But I've learned a lot by following Julia Child through long sequences; if what she has to say that I need to know were reduced to facing pages, it would be like trying to read the Lord's Prayer off the head of a pin. The obvious solution is to study *in advance* recipes that give detailed instructions as to procedure, not while in the throes of creation; we wouldn't expect to find Michelangelo on his scaffolding reading up on elementary pigmentation while trying to put the finishing touches on the fingers of God and Adam, would we?

Perhaps less forgivable than several-page recipes are those that are overly summarized, but even they may be excused in a cookbook that's supposed to be encyclopedic. The difficulty here, too, is in translating print into action. I have one cookbook that crams in recipes by lettering all the ingredients and numbering the steps of preparation, so that it resembles an algebra text, except that the letters are not lowercase and seldom get as far as x. Try following instructions like:

1. Peel and chop A, K, M, and O.
2. Add C, D, E, F, G, and H.
3. Marinate for 3 hours, then pour over J.
4. Whisk in I, stir L in carefully, and mix N with B and fold in gently.

At least the recipes can be found—some books bleed photographs out over where page numbers ought to be—and can be read, if not deciphered. The type, paper, and format of a good many cookbooks seem to have been chosen with a high aesthetic disregard for what the writer wanted to convey—some go along with nice bold type for all the peripheral stuff, for instance, then lapse into a spidery font for the recipes proper. I have a regional Italian cookbook that generally stays on the shelf, despite very fine recipes, because the paper is such a dark gray that the print blends right in. It's very soothing as long as you don't care what it says. And the pages are thick and of good quality; at least they *feel* better than the rough cheap paper of some books that you expect to turn yellow and begin falling apart when exposed to the light.

Of course, legibility may be in the eye of the beholder. No matter how clean the type and how well it stands out on whatever kind of paper, at the wrong distance from my glasses it's as frustrating as the anemic type so many recipes are printed in. If I ever get a holder that I have room for and can see into, my trifocals should work fine, since the middle part is set for me to read at about two-and-a-half feet. But with the books laid flat, I get mostly fuzz below and above a few clear lines. If I want to see a whole recipe clearly, I have to lean down close with my neck up, like a chicken drinking water, which not only makes my preparation time even slower than it would otherwise be but severely dissipates the effect on guests of the *Larousse* and *Gourmet* and Escoffier cookbooks aimed in their direction.

III

Settling In

> "Even the dumb creatures seemed to admire her in their own dumb way.
> The dumb rooks settled on her shoulder and every dumb dog around the place followed her."

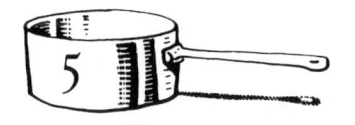

Not Yet the Hollandaise, Too Soon the Game Hens

If certain people will drop the charge that I am slow, I'll plead guilty to the lesser crime of being deliberate. I believe that carries a possible sentence of three to five, which, served at my rate, should take something like twelve to twenty. That ought to pay society totally for the delay Maurie and JoAnn suffered while I made the appetizer a few years ago, and in part for the subsequent raw Rock Cornish game hens.

If I weren't plea bargaining, I doubt that I would ever give out the details of that episode, not even to scatter the guilt about in an effort to obscure my own fault. There *were* accessories, of a sort, but I admit that I once blamed Julia Child more than I should have. For one thing, the cookbook that used such terms as "slowly" and "by droplets" in its recipe for hollandaise had two additional authors; who knows just how much culpability each should bear? Besides, I now realize that cookbook authors are like kindergarten teachers; most of their charges are on the verge of crashing into chairs or falling out of windows. They can't afford to give out as a general instruction, "Loosen up, for God's sake!" just because some deliberate kid takes fifteen minutes to arrange one alphabet block on top of another.

Deliberate, I still insist, not slow. I know myself clear back to childhood, and I can see the pattern. Take the only two times when I was a boy down South that I tried picking cotton. Each day I ended up with exactly thirteen pounds when everybody else was getting up toward a hundred. But mine was 100 percent pure unadulterated *cotton*. People said it was the cleanest they had ever seen, and that if everybody picked the way I did, cotton gins would go out of business.

Or take our neighbor Marge's tomato juice. I liked the Bloody Marys made with it so much that, some four or five years ago, I talked her into collaborating, on shares. She simmered great vats of tomatoes with peppers and onions and celery; my job was to run it all through her conical sieve with one of those wooden pestle-like things you roll around the inside.

"How much of the pulp should I press through?" I asked her.

"All you can," she said.

So I did. She sat there at her kitchen table a whole afternoon, waiting.

Why she didn't get up at least once and *look* I don't know, but she just smoked one cigarette after another till I got through, then came over, gasped, put out a tentative finger toward the bearded sieve, and said, "My God!" She thought for a minute that worms were coming out, but it was celery pulp in little white strings. There was only a handful of very dry pulp to throw away; the juice was so thick that guests would turn up their pre–football game Bloody Marys, wait a moment expectantly, hold them out at arm's length to study them, give them a good shaking, and try again. We thought of carving the celery sticks into spoons, but they would have broken off at the juice line.

Anyway, the hollandaise was deliberate—or I was deliberate about the hollandaise the same as I was about the tomato juice—but it was not a deliberate act of animosity or anything. In fact, as I said, I *sort* of blame Julia Child for it the same way I sort of blame Marge for saying "All you can" instead of describing it as all *she* could if she were doing it at her slapdash speed. I have to admit, though, that Julia and her coauthors did inform me, albeit in a rather disparaging tone, that hollandaise could be done in a blender by an eight-year-old.

"Let me do it," Candy in fact offered. "I've done it in the blender before, just like that." I don't remember whether she snapped her fingers or not. She had the Rock Cornish game hens all stuffed with pine nuts and waiting for the oven.

"Nothing to it," I said, pointing to "five minutes" in the book. "You do the entrée, I do the appetizer, remember?"

"Well, *you* remember that Maurie has one drink and then has to eat."

I wanted to do crabmeat Justine, which at Justine's restaurant in Memphis will make your tastebuds fairly curl up their toes with pleasure. My finished product didn't turn out so badly, either, considering that I had never dealt with crabmeat before, not to mention hollandaise. By the time it got done, anyway, everybody was too hungry to quibble over occasional bits of shell and gristle I hadn't known to pick out.

I left drinks up to Candy and had started to work by the time Maurie and JoAnn were seated. My intentions were above reproach. Heating the crabmeat mixture and putting it in ramekins was a matter of seconds. Minutes, at most. Then all I had to do was whip up the hollandaise to top it with. I got out my double boiler and wire whisk, started melting butter in a little pan, and was on my way. I thought I was moving along swiftly when Candy poked her head in the door and said, "Shouldn't I put the hens in the oven?" If we'd had the opening we've had cut since, she could have mouthed the question when nobody was looking.

I read my recipe again. "Not yet," I told her. "These have to go under the broiler first." We had only the one oven then. Electric. Broiler in the top. If I had known then what I know now, I'd have let her stick the things in to get broiled, baked, roasted—whatever heat we could have put to them—but I didn't.

"Well, hurry," she said. "Maurie's already reaching for his Gelusil."

I glanced around the corner, and sure enough, there was his hand sneaking up to his mouth. That was the last I saw of anybody for what must have been hours.

Here I have to shift to Candy's version of what happened. I could tell my side of the story by writing "dribble and whisk" five hundred times on the blackboard. Candy says that after a good while they gave up all efforts at talk; sound was reduced to the clink of ice in her desperate third drink punctuated by an occasional plop as Maurie now openly popped Gelusil tablets into his mouth. From the kitchen there would be a little chip-chip-chip flurry of the whisk in the heavy porcelain double boiler, then a long silence during which

Candy would think, At last, he's putting them in the oven. But no; again the brief chip-chip-chip; again a long silence.

Finally she could sit there no longer. She marched into the kitchen all ready to whisper something fairly pungent, but what met her eye stalled all comment. The kitchen, she says, looked like the laboratory of some B-movie mad scientist, with pans toppling this way and that in tall stacks. Butter dripped from everything; egg yolk was splattered all over the place. My eyes were glazed, my shirttail was out, and what hair I have was in damp little tendrils around my ears. "Poor thing," she said instead. "It'll turn out all right."

It didn't. The gritty crabmeat might have allayed and sharpened appetites if it had come a decade or so earlier, but after that, too, there was the long wait while the Rock Cornish game hens pretended to be cooking. Candy is no great shakes of a cook, but it wasn't her fault. I mean, she does the best prime rib in the country, and she can grill a steak okay, and that's about it. But she had worked hard to do something different and had in fact tried the Rock Cornish hens with pine nut stuffing before with excellent results. She hasn't done them since, but nobody has requested them, either.

The oven did it to her. Never before had that oven failed us, but for some reason, even with the heating unit blazing red, it didn't *cook*. When the buzzer went off, the little birds were still as cheerful as Shadrach, Meshach, and Abednego in Nebuchadnezzar's fiery furnace. She turned up the thermostat, set the timer for fifteen more minutes, and came back to the silent group with no more color in her face than the hens had acquired.

After a second overtime, there was nothing to do but declare the damn things done and get on with it. It was well past Maurie's bedtime by then, and anyway the Rock Cornish game hens were vaguely warm, despite the frigid globs that filled their cavities. Poor JoAnn, trying valiantly to keep civility intact, chattered away solo as we pulled and tugged at the raw meat, but of course—the way we find ourselves inevitably punctuating whatever we say to blind people with Don't you see?—she couldn't extricate herself from an account of a "gourmet" acquaintance who served up one tasteless dish after another.

We've stayed friends—I suppose that people who face near starvation together forge unbreakable bonds—but more often than not we wind up at their house for dinner. Even though I have become, over the years, a truly accomplished cook, they do have a basement rec room and a swimming pool, and we don't.

Marge didn't let one little incident spoil our visits to and fro over the back fence, either. She would have even done tomato juice again, after we chewed our way through that one batch, if the next summer hadn't been too dry for much of a crop, and the one after that so wet that, as she put it, the tomatoes were nothing but water. Last fall she brought over a quart of excellent tomato juice for pre–football game Bloody Marys, but I think she was telling the truth when she said it was from half-a-dozen years back and had just gotten overlooked behind something in the basement.

With practice, I've made myself much more efficient in the kitchen, too. Now I ask Candy well in advance when she wants dinner, and if she says, "Eight-thirty," I plan everything out in my head and start in plenty of time, so that we are nearly always eating by a quarter past nine. Candy says I'm wrong in referring to the difference as a margin for error, but whatever you call it, it doesn't amount to much. Besides, I happen to think *she's* wrong to attribute it to a kind of invincible inability to deal with the exigencies of time, which is how I interpret her less articulate "not very bright." It's really the result of perdurable optimism, and I think that if there were more optimistic and deliberate people in the world it would be a better place in which to sit around and wait to eat.

MARGE'S TOMATO JUICE

When eventually I called Marge and asked what her recipe was for making tomato juice, she was surprised to find one in her file. It was set up for only 2 gallons of tomatoes; she thought she had probably just guessed the time we cooked them up by the vatload. She read it to me:

"It says to use

2 gallons tomatoes, skinned and cut in sections
2 cups chopped celery
1 cup chopped green pepper
1 cup chopped onion
2 ½ teaspoons salt

and simmer about an hour, but I do it longer, and there's no need to skin the tomatoes, is there, if you're going to run them through the sieve? Oh, and squeeze through only a little of the pulp, it says." The recipe should give you about five or six quarts, if the tomatoes aren't too watery and you don't over-squeeze.

BLOODY MARYS

I learned to make Bloody Marys from my friend Robin so many years ago that I'm not sure how much resemblance mine now bear to the originals. One change I know I made is from store-bought tomato juice to Marge's, when I can get it. If none of hers is available, I use V-8 juice. One thing I'm sure I haven't changed is the amount of Worcestershire sauce: "Pour it in," Robin told me, "until you think you have too much, then add some more."

The order of procedure is important. First put

A few ice cubes

into a tumbler, filling it no more than halfway. Next pour in

1 jigger vodka

Now comes

Worcestershire sauce (use Lea & Perrins—others taste different)

The idea is to darken the vodka until it loses all watery appearance. You're more likely to use too little than too much. Squeeze and drop in

$1/_{12}$ section lime

(Cut lime in two across the middle, cut halves in two, then cut fourths into three pieces each.) Add

A sprinkling of garlic powder
A few grains of salt
A couple of grinds of black pepper

Also add

> *5 drops Tabasco*

if you can take it hot; otherwise, reduce the Tabasco to your level. Add

> *V-8 juice*

until the glass is full, stir until the Worcestershire sauce no longer shows as dark swirls, stick in a stalk of celery, and be sure to give a mental toast to Robin, as I do every time I hoist one.

CRABMEAT JUSTINE

I have yet to make this appetizer come out just exactly the way it is served at Justine's, but even so it is delicious and I keep edging closer. Next time I intend to try soaking bread crumbs in a little sherry and putting a few on top to be browned under the broiler along with the hollandaise. Candy thinks something like that will give it the immediate flavor we seem to get at Justine's, along with the old Memphis atmosphere and linen tablecloths and heavy silver and marvelous service; not a single waiter has ever come up to us, there, and said, "Hi! My name is Rick, and I'm your waiter for the evening." Instead, you are *waited on*, if you know what I mean, and left to enjoy the company and the food you obviously wanted to concentrate on for the evening, else why wouldn't you have taken Rick out to McDonald's, or something?

Have ready

1 cup fresh lump crabmeat
½ stick butter
1 hard-boiled egg, grated
2 tablespoons sherry
1 ½ teaspoons fresh lemon juice
Tabasco
4 squares toast
hollandaise sauce (see p. 35)

Melt butter; add crabmeat, grated egg, sherry, lemon juice, and a couple of dashes of Tabasco. Heat thoroughly, allowing the liquid to evaporate. Spoon onto toast squares in four heated ramekins. Top with hollandaise sauce (and maybe try those bread crumbs soaked in sherry), and run under broiler until browned. Serve immediately.

One aspect of the recipe I have copied as it is in *The Memphis Cookbook* (a contribution of Mrs. Dayton Smith, who is Justine), even though I have never tried it that way. Here in mid-Ohio, not once when I have decided to do this recipe have I been able to find fresh crabmeat. Maybe that's the only thing that makes mine turn out a little different. It couldn't be the quality of the chef at Justine's, of course.

ROCK CORNISH GAME HENS with PINE NUT STUFFING
(An If-You-Really-Want-to-Try-It Recipe)

The recipe for the little hens that wouldn't cook has long since disappeared. I think it may have gone up in spontaneous combustion while the hens stayed cold that night, or perhaps it is a victim of self-immolation. Anyway, this is a new one I invented for anyone who might be challenged by our failure. When I tried it, the hens colored up nicely and got done throughout, and all that. And the flavors are really good. The thing is, I'm afraid we don't really care for Rock Cornish game hens, done or not: It is just too hard to eat them, and it's almost impossible to get at the stuffing in their little bone-protected cavities. Nevertheless, in case somebody out there insists:

R.C.G.H. with P.N.S.

THE STUFFING
In a small pot, boil down till nearly dry

1 small shallot, minced
1 teaspoon dried tarragon
½ cup white wine

allow to cool. Stir in

2 tablespoons softened butter
5 or 6 drops Tabasco

and hold the mixture aside.

In a larger pot, stir together

½ *cup brown rice*
1 scant cup stock, or scant cup water including 2 tablespoons meat glaze (see p. 170)
½ tablespoon butter
A pinch of salt

Bring rice and liquid to a boil; cover, reduce heat to very low, and cook for 45 minutes. Turn off heat; let sit, covered, until cool enough to work with.

Stir into rice

Shallot mixture (above)
½ cup pine nuts, toasted
2 tablespoons slivered almonds, toasted

THE HENS

4 to 6 Rock Cornish game hens
2 to 3 cloves garlic, pressed
Salt
Freshly ground black pepper

Rinse hens in cold water; dry with paper towels. Rub pressed garlic and sprinkle salt and pepper into cavities; fill loosely with rice and pine nut stuffing; truss.

Brush hens with a mixture of

2 tablespoons butter, melted
2 tablespoons lemon juice

Put hens in shallow pan, breast side up, and bake at 375 degrees for thirty minutes. Baste with butter and lemon juice, then lower heat to 350 degrees and continue cooking for another thirty minutes, basting as you see fit. Either saw the little birds in half before serving or leave them a feast for the eyes and let your guests struggle for sustenance.

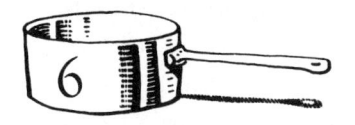

Allegro, Ma Non Troppo

A few years ago, when my friend Murray began to try a little cooking of his own—possibly because he figured he couldn't do any worse than I did with the cannelloni I'd fed him and Nancy so inadequately—he said in awe about a cook who had been at it for years, "She can turn her back to the stove!" He told me, too, about a cookbook in which the author, after trying to explain a procedure two or three different ways, wrote down her telephone number and something like, "If you get this far and can't figure out what to do, call me."

It's not easy to get into writing just how to give raw ingredients their trial by fire and have them come out with the right texture and color and flavor. That's why so many recipes settle for "cook till done" and why the cook who can't yet turn his back on the stove breaks out in a cold sweat. "Till *done?*" he's likely to shout, as if he could be heard across the miles and years. "Give me a clue!"

He needs more than a clue. Try the one that's perhaps most common: "Sauté slowly until golden." In the world of sentimental fiction, every little girl has golden tresses; in the fictional world of recipes, nearly anything edible turns golden when the heat is on. I have watched various foods go from sort of off-white all the way to black while I waited in vain for something resembling what people wear on their fingers or in their earlobes or around their wrists. I've seen things turn speckled, beige, tan, brown, and even, I seem to recall about a scallop of veal, mauve, but hardly what I consider "golden" or even that slight compromise "golden brown."

When I began reading recipes for practical purposes, I tended to skip over those that used terms I wasn't sure of; there were millions that said "grill," which I thought I understood, so why bother with "braise," or "fricassee"? Part of what I didn't know was that familiarity with the term doesn't have a whole lot to do with execution of the process; grilling over charcoal requires at least as much skill as does braising, and not just because it's harder to control the heat. If a backyard specialist hadn't shown me, I wouldn't have guessed that you put barbecue sauce on ribs only toward the last. It was fortunate that I hadn't tried them; the crust of burnt sauce over half-cooked meat would probably have resulted in, if not trichinosis, indigestion so severe as to preclude all further relationship with "grill."

When I began to try to put recipes on paper for others to work from, it became apparent that there is no way, short of giving your phone number, to satisfy the different levels and areas of ignorance. You can't explain every word in every recipe on the off chance that somebody may not be acquainted with it. One person admitted to me having been stymied by "shortening." I thought everybody knew what shortening was. That's one thing I grew up knowing, perhaps from having heard "Short'nin' Bread" sung on the radio by Nelson Eddy several dozen times, or from being around the kitchen while my mother was at work, or maybe just from reading Crisco labels.

It was from reading books that I had learned a little esoterica by the time Nina, my daughter, called to ask, "What do they mean by the zest of a lemon?" When I told her it was the yellow part of the peel, she broke into laughter. "I couldn't find anything that told me," she said, "so I figured that it meant all the part that had flavor."

"Oh?" I said. "What did you do?"

"I just threw in the whole lemon."

There are enough such quasi-obscure terms in current American recipes to stop beginners and give us intermediates occasional pause, but the older cookbooks and those translated from other languages, cultures, and cuisines are full of hitches and halts. How much is "a wineglass," as a measure? What to do when "aubergine" is translated from French as "aubergine"? I ran across a set of recipes recently that called for chicken cutlets, and it was only when Irene, who was fortunately along, pointed out that the heading for the series was "Suprêmes de Volaille" that I was able to go from what I presume is English through French to American, and hence to what might result in food on the table.

Many years in the classroom on both sides of the desk have convinced me that teaching is nearly always corrective, mostly aimed at either curbing excess lack of control or loosening up those who are bound too tight, hoping that they'll quit confining themselves to rote and begin using at least a modicum of their own initiative. One reason it's a good thing that students pay so little attention to their teachers is that out-of-control kids in a class taught by a "creative" teacher are being urged in effect to go completely berserk, and orderly children taught by an authoritarian are being mustered into faceless platoons.

That's why I had trouble with "drop by drop" in a hollandaise-sauce recipe, since I was already overly deliberate, but came through immediately with "stir-fry and remove," because it forced me to quit trying to do it exactly by the book. When I took up tennis after thirty years off and decided to learn it "right," I tried so hard to follow instructions (cocked my wrist just so, took my racket back on the proper plane, moved my left foot forward, and so on) that the ball would pass me approximately forty-eight seconds before I got my parts in place to hit it. I finally learned that I had to hit the ball however I could and try to correct my swing—at least this way I got to swing—one aspect at a time. Compulsive lungers at the ball, on the other hand, need a pro to nail down their feet, cock their wrists, and force the racquet through the proper arc slowly enough for the idea and feel of it to sink in.

Of course, each of us has within us the too-orderly and the too-loose in varying doses about various things. I may be too rigid on the tennis court and too orderly in the kitchen, but my desk is chaos itself. No man is all of a piece, as Somerset Maugham has pointed out more than once, and the poor writer of recipes can't possibly know which part of which person is being addressed, and so in which direction to be corrective.

That's why both ways may be the only way. I took up golf, too, even later than tennis, and at first, when I would play with Candy's father, I had a tendency to laugh when he would instruct me as I was about to putt. Now, I see that he's like the composer who notes that a movement should be *Allegro, ma non troppo*: it's as good as any way of saying that there is no way of saying just exactly how spirited it should be, and, like Candy's father's "Now, hit it hard enough. You've got to get it there," followed after a second or two by "But not too hard," it does at least make you concentrate on feeling out the tempo. I mean, even if he could judge the needed pressure exactly, "Give it x ounces of stroke" wouldn't help, since I am not a calibrated machine. Nobody can give you a precise formula for art, anyway, and if music and golf and cooking aren't art, then what is?

STIR-FRYING

Most stir-fry dishes are set up to serve two people; instead of tripling The Jewels of Mei Tang Poo, for example, to feed six, both the Chinese and the mock Chinese method is to add two other dishes: ribs, for instance, or a chicken stir-fry, along with fried rice.

It is often easier to improvise a stir-fry than to follow a recipe, although I'd advise doing a few standard dishes first to get an idea of how much meat of what kind in what size and shape you want to stir together with what sauce materials in what proportions, and what vegetables, in what order.

My usual approach is to run variations on the following: For beef, use a one-pound-plus flank steak in quarter-inch slices; for chicken, two whole breasts, boned, trimmed, and cut into bite-sized cubes. That's twice as much meat as many Chinese recipes indicate; perhaps we're more carnivorous than we should be.

Since the marinade and the sauce start out identically, I set out two small bowls and make them at the same time: Each begins with a teaspoon of cornstarch (which helps the marinade cling to the meat and, in the sauce, serves as a thickening as well as binding agent); dissolve it in two tablespoons of soy sauce plus two tablespoons of either gin or a fairly dry sherry.

Since the marinade is to enhance the flavor of the meat (it should be stirred in at least twenty minutes before cooking begins), soy and spirits are generally enough. The sauce, which goes in last, brings the whole dish together with subtle and complex flavors achieved by adding one or more of the following: a tablespoon or more of oyster sauce or half that amount of hoisin sauce, a teaspoon of sesame oil, a teaspoon of sesame seeds, a couple of chopped green onions, a teaspoon or more of minced fresh ginger, or whatever pops into mind and sounds good at the time. Sometimes I use not only, say, oyster sauce and ginger and sesame oil and hot oil but also things like fermented black beans, rinsed, drained, and mashed—perhaps two tablespoons of these if I have a taste for pungency—and sometimes a quarter or half teaspoon of crushed red pepper, if hot is my desire.

The wok should be on high heat throughout, unless you need to lower the flame momentarily while fumbling to add more oil after the meat is removed. Let the empty wok get quite hot, then swirl in about two tablespoons of oil, so that it coats the lower sides of the wok as well as gathers in the bottom, and bring it almost to smoking. (How, for the love of God, are you supposed to know when it's *almost* smoking? Well, you watch it carefully as it gets *to* smoking a time or two, and then you'll see the way the oil begins to work before it gets there. Trial and error, with error necessary—as irritating to us perfectionists as that may be.)

If raw cashews or peanuts are to be part of the dish, put them in now and let them crisp up; remove with a slotted spoon and hold till later. If you're using walnuts, they do best blanched and dried before being fried. Also, you may want to flavor the oil with a couple of cloves of peeled garlic; let them just start to change color before removing them with the slotted spoon and tossing them into the disposal.

In goes the marinated meat, to be stirred and tossed until it loses most of its pink if it's beef or turns fully opaque if it's chicken. Remove, add a bit more oil to the wok if necessary, let it get hot again (a film of cornstarch will be browning sort of crustily, but ignore it; it will soak off afterward), and, if you're doing hot stuff, maybe throw in two to four dried hot peppers and let them turn rather black before reprising your slotted-spoon toss into the disposal.

Now for the vegetables; they must have been prepared in advance, because once you're cooking there are no time-outs. Most vegetables do best cut diagonally, to expose more surface; fresh mushrooms I cut into quarters or sixths, according to size. The least delicate vegetables should go into the heated oil first; frozen snow peas, if you're using them, can go in now and be thawed and cooked in a minute or so, until they sort of green up a little; fresh snow peas can go in with things like carrots, bell peppers, celery, or bok choy; stir-fry for a moment before adding water chestnuts or bean sprouts or pimento or black olives or mushrooms. These take only seconds of stirring and tossing before the meat goes back in along with any nuts you might be using and, of course, the sauce—after giving it a quick final stir so that the cornstarch isn't left silted out on the bottom of the bowl. By this time it is a matter of keeping the whole mess in motion only until the sauce clarifies and thickens nicely, scraping it out onto a platter, and digging in.

The JEWELS of MEI TANG POO

Since "stir-fry and remove" came so naturally to me, I soon found myself inventing my own stir-fry recipes. I'd usually concoct the dish, with Candy as color consultant, and then she would come up with the names, like Jungle Chicken, or The Paintbox of the Foreign Artist, or Confusion Blossoms in the New Year. "The Jewels of Mei Tang Poo" is from the last line of a parody by Noël Coward, so what I'm about to describe is really a mock Chinese dish with a mock Chinese name from a mock translation of a mock Chinese poem.

This is the revised standard version; the King James, so to speak, appeared in *A Man's Taste* a few years ago, but of course I've been unable to keep from fooling with the marinade and the sauce, and here I've indicated fresh red bell peppers instead of canned pimentos—which can be used, however, if fresh red bell peppers are not available.

For sauce, combine and hold aside in a small dish

2 tablespoons soy sauce
2 tablespoons gin
1 teaspoon cornstarch
1 teaspoon sesame oil
1 tablespoon oyster sauce
2 or 3 drops hot oil

Cut

1 to 1½ pounds flank steak into ¼-inch slices across the grain; slices should be 2 to 3 inches long (partially freezing the meat helps in cutting it thin)

Marinate flank steak in

> 2 tablespoons soy sauce
> 2 tablespoons gin
> 1 teaspoon cornstarch
> A couple of drops of garlic juice squeezed from press

Stir-fry flank steak in

> 2 tablespoons oil

and remove.

Stir-fry

> 1 package frozen snow peas

till thawed. Add

> 1 can whole water chestnuts, drained
> 2 small red bell peppers, cut into 1-inch squares

and continue to stir-fry briefly.

Return flank steak to wok. Stir sauce ingredients again briefly and add them, too. Stir-fry till warm and thickened. Serve with rice. This makes plenty for two or three, according to the size of the flank steak.

CONFUSION BLOSSOMS in the NEW YEAR

Remember to have all the ingredients ready before starting to cook: the chicken cut up and marinated, the sauce ingredients combined and stirred, the nuts measured and waiting, the vegetables chopped and piled onto a plate, the orange sliced into wedges, and a platter warmed.

Marinate

2 whole chicken breasts, boned, skinned, and diced

in

2 tablespoons soy sauce
1 teaspoon cornstarch
2 tablespoons sherry
1 teaspoon sesame oil

Combine (and have waiting) for sauce

2 tablespoons soy sauce
1 teaspoon cornstarch
2 tablespoons gin
2 tablespoons oyster sauce
A pinch of ground ginger

In

2 tablespoons corn oil

stir-fry

> 2 *tablespoons or more pine nuts*
> 2 *tablespoons or more slivered almonds*

Remove and hold aside nuts. Add and stir-fry chicken; remove and hold aside. Add and stir-fry

> ½ *green bell pepper, cut in strips*
> 2 *carrots, sliced diagonally*
> 2 *stalks celery, sliced diagonally*
> 3 *dried mushrooms, soaked 20 minutes, drained, squeezed dry, and sliced*

Return chicken and nuts to wok along with sauce (give it a quick last stir to suspend cornstarch again); stir-fry until sauce is clarified and thickens to your taste; remove to warm platter; garnish with

> *1 orange, washed and sliced into 12 wedges*

Serve with rice. Feeds two hungry people.

Before anyone mars it with a serving utensil, remark on what nice colors it has, and, as you eat, comment on the texture—how crunchy the almonds are, how crisp the vegetables—and on the impressive array of flavors. Do so mentally, of course, unless you don't mind being a bit obnoxious, but with enough intensity to get through to your guests in case ESP should prove to be a valid concept.

IV

Vigil 'Neath the Casement

"He was sitting on a thorn bush, . . . and his upturned face wore an expression of agonized pallor."

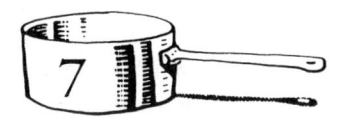

# Upstaged

It was inevitable, I suppose, that Maurie would throw one of my most audacious dishes-for-company askew and then completely eclipse it with a skittle top. He had suffered through the two-hour hollandaise and raw Rock Cornish game hens; taking over my potatoes came nowhere near getting me back for that. Then, too, there is just the nature of the man, which we should have known skittles would bring to some sort of apotheosis.

We may say it's for dinner, but whenever Candy and I get together with Maurie and JoAnn and their son T. J., we either start out or end up—sometimes both—trying our damnedest to outdo each other at some game, real or imagined. In cold or rainy weather, at their house, it's killer Ping-Pong in the basement rec room. From Memorial Day to Labor Day it's volleyball in the shallow end of their swimming pool, without a net. We tried it with the net for a while, but that tended to limit competition to while the ball was in play.

Let me observe that all of our group were born competitors (although I, of course, keep it in perspective), and, without calling names, that one among us has kept on the burner a fierce determination never to lose for longer than the three score and ten years the Bible arbitrarily allots us. To get some idea of what he's like, bring to a boil in cognac some good strong shallots and garlic, some highly concentrated *glace de viande*, some vinegar, some mustard, cayenne, Tabasco, a chopped-up pickle, some capers, a little minced ham—simmer that for seventy-some-odd years. Stir in a little softened butter for a sort of deceptive bedside manner—he is, after all, an M.D.—but don't put your poached fillet of sole up against it.

Who could beat, for a touch of butter, his prescription for my fingers' tendency to go numb? "Do me a favor," he said, "and try a shot of whiskey." Do *him* a favor? But ask him about a hypodermic needle, "What's in that?" and you'll get, "Shut up and bend over." When Candy went to him with the flu a while back, he told her, "Don't let Bob get it. I don't want to see him. He's the ugliest person in the world when he's sick."

A man like that you either let take over your potatoes or you don't. At netless volleyball, he can take over a point before you have time to realize that the spike he tried to make would have left a hole in the net, if it had been there, like a cannonball through a chicken-wire fence. How he retrieves the ball and gets it back to his server so quickly, I don't know. He should have been a surgeon. Or a magician: I'll get to the skittle top in a minute. It's not in the hornets' nest for sure, although for it to have buzzed right in would be appropriate in all kinds of ways; there's only the one hole, and it's too small. I've measured.

T. J. is a chip off the old block, or a chunk, rather. He's still a growing boy, but he shows signs of ending up as big as Maurie and JoAnn put together. He can, and will, serve a Ping-Pong ball so hard it fairly cracks against the wall behind you while you still think you're getting ready. And JoAnn has assimilated a lot, too. Her forte is the massive serve at volleyball—at the very mention of which game she and Maurie become Big Mama and Big Daddy, despite their size.

But Maurie is the daddy of us all. It goes way back. He's the only person I know who didn't hang around until somewhere close to his teens, but ran away from home—not just down the block or till almost suppertime—at the age of three. Or maybe it was eight. But *little*. And tough. Fought in the ring at the lower weights. Smaller than any golfer on the tour, but used to go for the green off the tee on par fours, and sometimes make it. Still busting ribs on and off his horse under trees and over jumps at the hunt club. I really don't think he meant to do away with that skittle top; I think he just couldn't help it.

I think, too, that it did have something to do with getting us back for the hollandaise and game hens; even though I think he knows I didn't *mean* to starve him that night, waiting around to eat is not something Maurie does willingly. Once when we went to their house for dinner, we got the time wrong by half an hour and stayed a course behind right on through dessert.

Anyway, you can understand why, even though in the intervening years I had developed my skills in the kitchen considerably, Maurie should insist on helping me cook when they were over some three or four years ago. I don't let just anybody in my kitchen, but it would have been difficult to say no to Maurie, even if I had thought I could make it stick.

This time I was showing off with suprêmes de volaille à la bordelaise after Escoffier, and while I was sautéeing the chicken breasts in one pan and the sliced artichoke hearts in another and steaming a side dish of asparagus in still another, I let Maurie sauté the thinly sliced potatoes for me.

"Those potatoes are to be mixed with the artichoke hearts and bound with a little meat glaze," I thought it best to explain. I don't usually talk like that, but I thought that sounding like a cookbook might lend an air of authority. "Then we'll mold that into a base for the chicken."

Maurie may or may not have nodded. He was absorbed in the potatoes, turning the slices one at a time, his face downright beatific. I had thought that, after the night of the hollandaise, he had simply wanted to be sure he got something done enough to eat before morning, but I could tell now that some inner zeal had taken over my potatoes.

"I mean," I told Maurie, "you want to get them *done*, of course, but not *too* done. Nothing like hash browns, you know?"

Maurie kept turning the slices in what I guess you'd call a culinary trance. They were coloring up more than I'd intended, but with all the guilt about the hollandaise, and with his so obvious pleasure in wielding the spatula, I couldn't bring myself to say, "That's *enough*." Besides, Maurie's older than I am, and he's my doctor. There are those couple or three times, too, when I've waked him in the middle of the night and didn't die or anything to prove it was serious.

The potatoes were evenly browned and perfectly crisp when Maurie turned off the heat, cocked an eye up at me, and said, "I make a great chocolate mousse."

Regardless of what Escoffier had in mind, the potatoes worked all right with the artichoke hearts and meat glaze. I thought it was a pretty elegant meal, and although Maurie's potatoes drew the only admiring remarks, I took them as the kind of compliment you'd pay a novice sous-chef, reflecting even greater glory upon his superior.

My memory of dessert is rather vague now, but I think I served pêches

Melba before we got down to what the others seemed to have been waiting for all along.

We have neither a rec room nor a pool, so games at our house are of the table-top variety. We had tried Hungry, Hungry Hippos, where each person presses a lever to make his plastic hippo lunge forward, raise its upper and only jaw, and try to grab the marbles let loose, supposedly one at a time, by the players in turn. The problem was that we never got half a dozen marbles out before Maurie couldn't stand it any longer and began flipping out marbles and banging away at his hippo—with everybody else a feverish half second behind—like an old-time gunslinger fanning his hammer. We changed the name of the game to the title of the little Boynton book, *Hippos Go Berserk*, but by then it had degenerated into such raw undifferentiated competitive chaos that there was no way to score.

So we took up skittles. For anyone who doesn't already know, skittles is played within the confines (except by Candy and T. J. occasionally, and Maurie the one time I'm leading up to) of a large wooden boxlike structure sectioned off at each end into little roofless rooms with "doors" cut between them and out onto what you might call the ballroom floor. An opening from the outside is cut in the center room at one end, through which the player may hold a skittle top with his finger and pull a string to send it spinning. It is supposed to go forth and knock down skittles, or wooden tenpins. A skittle top is not so deep as a well nor so wide as a church door, but neither is it so small that it could escape notice and get itself vacuumed up. It is a wooden wheel a half inch thick and an inch and a half across, to be exact, with a nearly three-inch axle on which to spin.

They say that dogs take on certain characteristics of their masters. I know that skittle tops do. T. J.'s tended to go straight out the door of the little room, if it didn't leap over, and zap-zap-zap from one side to the other, bouncing the five- and ten-point pins off the walls. Big Mama's (they started that with skittles, too) would bore straight down the floor and force its way into the far rooms to get at the fifties, and through them into the center room for the lone hundred. Candy's would go off like a frightened buzz saw, angling frantically up and sometimes over the walls, laying waste with a roar to everything. Mine, no matter what I tried, would stay perfectly upright, spinning sedately and quietly along between pins until it went into a little reclining circular spasm, without disturbing anything.

Maurie's top that night, for some reason, kept lunging from one side room to the other, sort of chewing up the minus pins. I think that's why he finally cut a longer piece of very stout string. We'd broken all of Candy's kite string, and what we had begun using was about as close to rope as you can wind around the stem of a skittle top.

What happened then we are all witness to. Not only do we watch each other at such a game like blue jays set to swoop down upon a marauding cat, but we are obliged to be a part of every play to keep the skittle box from plunging to the floor. Our dining table, which we had cleared for the occasion, is not completely steady in the first place, but even on solid rock we'd have to hold the sides to offset the violence of every pull. So we all saw Maurie wind the string, ease it down through the slot cut for it, place the top inside the little room, put his finger upon it the way we used to hold a football for the kickoff—all this with the rhythm and pace of a good slow backswing in golf—and then, with the proper acceleration of a downswing that sweeps the ball from under your eye at just the peak of force, pull.

We had become adept at controlling the skittle box, rather like a set of heavy-duty shock absorbers, and I think the first thing we were aware of was that the skittles scarcely quivered upon their slender bases. Then that nothing had leapt aside into one of the rooms to gnaw upon a minus skittle. Then that nothing was going on at all.

Maurie was standing there with the string hanging limp from one hand, face bemused, as if waiting for his skittle top to get out there and start scoring for him, but *there was no skittle top*. It simply wasn't there. After a sort of inane moment of inertia, we began to look around as though it had somehow silently flown over the walls and silently landed somewhere, but I think that, deep down, every one of us knew we'd never see that skittle top again.

We searched for it, all right—behind, in, and under every piece of furniture and every houseplant, on top of the central beam that runs along just under the low peak of the ceiling, all over and into the big hornets' nest Candy hung from the beam for decoration after I had gotten it down from the maple tree beside our garage. Don't think we didn't check Maurie's pockets, sleeves, lapels, and socks, either. We *felt* over the walls and carpet out in front of and beside where Maurie was standing, and then even in the area behind him, to reach which it would have had to go through his body.

I had intended, of course, for the evening to be memorable for my resurrection of an Escoffier dish you don't find on every menu in central Ohio—who besides me in the whole state puts in the two or three days over a hot stove to make just the meat glaze? But instead of remembering suprêmes de volaille à la bordelaise, we were left, absurd as it may seem for four grown people and one who is the physical and mental equivalent of grown—gourmets, too, we all fancy ourselves—obsessed with and haunted by a skittle top.

It was a couple of years before Candy and I could walk through that part of the house without the wary feeling that if we didn't look directly at wherever it might be, maybe we'd see it. If we went to Maurie for a sore throat, the first question he'd ask was, "Did you ever find that skittle top?" The summer after its disappearance, they spent a month in a villa in Spain, and JoAnn told us when they got back that, even there, whenever the phone rang she just knew we were calling to say that we had found it.

I can't speak for the others, but I never see a story whose headline mentions Path of Destruction without expecting it to quote some sheriff's deputy as saying, "You wouldn't believe that a little skittle top could come out of nowhere and wipe out a whole trailer park," to which my silent response would be, Not unless you knew it was put into orbit by Big Daddy, you wouldn't.

UPSTAGED MENU

If I remember correctly, the menu for the evening Maurie did whatever he did to the skittle top went something like this:

Chilled Consommé Madrilène
Suprêmes de Volaille à la Bordelaise
Salade Verte
Pêches Melba

Correct or not, that wouldn't be a bad program for an evening. We did have wine, of course, and I'm sure it was some sort of white, but what we were drinking then I have no idea. Roger the Vintner keeps me stocked with a succession of excellent inexpensive wines; my only advice on the subject is: Get yourself a Roger.

CHILLED CONSOMMÉ MADRILÈNE

All I do to make a madrilène is thaw out enough of the stock I keep frozen (see p. 170) for as many bowls as we'll be serving, add a good coloring of V-8 (I'm partial to it) or tomato juice, and, for each serving, a dash or two of Tabasco and Worcestershire sauce, plus a teaspoon or so of dry sherry. Chill it in the bowls until jelled, and top it with a sprig of parsley or a curl of pimento, or both. Good rich stock is what makes it tasty.

SUPRÊMES de VOLAILLE
à la BORDELAISE

Although we usually eat a whole chicken breast each, gourmands that we are, with this rather rich recipe, and with the soup and salad and dessert, half that much will do. What holds the dish together is the meat glaze, and the secret of that is a lot of time and a fair amount of attention. I think it is worth it, but, you know, twice a year? At most?

For half a dozen people (we don't cook for more, or the table divides itself into smaller groups, and I wouldn't do this meal for fewer):

3 whole chicken breasts, skinned, boned, and halved
Salt
Freshly ground black pepper
6 tablespoons unsalted butter, divided
3 or 4 potatoes
3 fresh artichokes
4 tablespoons meat glaze (see p. 171), divided
4 tablespoons dry white wine
4 tablespoons stock (see p. 170)

Season the breast halves with a little salt and pepper, and sauté them in 2 tablespoons butter until done and nicely colored. Set them aside in a warm place. Peel the potatoes, slice them thin, and, in another pan, sauté them in 2 more tablespoons butter until tender; add a sprinkling of salt. Trim the artichokes down to their bottoms (see below); slice the bottoms thin and, in yet another pan, sauté them in 1 tablespoon butter until just tender; add a touch of salt. The potatoes will take longer than the artichokes, so time yourself accordingly. Mix potatoes and artichokes, bind with half the meat glaze, mold into six mounds on a serving platter, and put the sautéed chicken breast halves on top.

Turn up the heat under the pan the chicken was cooked in, with its butter and leavings still there, and deglaze with the wine, scraping and stirring. Bring to a boil; add the stock and the rest of the meat glaze; boil for a brief moment; take off the heat and stir in the remaining tablespoon of butter; pour over the chicken; serve. Accept compliments, unless Maurie is there to upstage you.

If it suits your style, you may want to set up the mounds on your guests' individual plates; it's easier that way. Nothing is easy about getting the bottoms out of artichokes, although practice makes it not too difficult. With a sharp heavy knife, being very careful not to let it slip, cut off the top part of the leaves. Pull away the truncated leaves with your fingers; dig out the choke with a spoon; use a sharp paring knife to trim around the bottom where the pulled leaves have left their stumps; cut off the stem. Rub the bottom all over with lemon to keep it from discoloring, and wait until just before cooking to slice it.

Canned, frozen, or marinated artichoke bottoms or hearts might be easier, but if you're going to the trouble to make stock and meat glaze, don't shy away from a bit more work and end up without the dish you've worked so hard to make.

SALADE VERTE

Well, really, salad made of mostly raw green stuff. We generally break up one or more of the following: leaf lettuce, red leaf lettuce, spinach, Boston lettuce, Bibb lettuce, romaine. According to what the main dish is, what our taste buds call for, and what's in the house, we add carrot slices and/or mushroom chunks and/or bits of oil-cured black olives and/or bits of Sicilian green olives and/or, and/or, and/or . . . well, celery, avocado chunks marinated in lemon juice, bell pepper (red and/or green), a bit of minced fresh hot pepper, prosciutto, toasted pine nuts, toasted slivered almonds, some sort of cheese—whatever. But I do have a kind of basic dressing.

Into a little bowl, pour enough

Extra-virgin olive oil

to moisten well as many bowlfuls of salad as you'll be serving.
Add

About $1/8$ as much red wine vinegar as olive oil
About as much Dijon mustard as vinegar
About twice the measure of finely minced parsley, or whatever fresh herbs
 you have, as vinegar
White pepper, to your taste
Sweet paprika, to your taste
A touch of garlic from the press

Whisk with a fork until emulsified.

A Greek-like salad, to go with a menu that can take it (not the upstaged meal), is distinguished from any other green salad by the addition of watercress, hard-boiled egg, and Calamata olive pieces to the body and a little anchovy paste and thyme to the dressing. Feta chunks don't hurt anything, either.

These have been staple salads with us for some time, and when Velma, Candy's mother, announced a while back that she was serving a Mandarin salad, both Candy and I winced. We should have licked our chops. It would have been good even with the upstaged dinner, if we had known about it in time.

VELMA'S MANDARIN SALAD

THE SALAD

1 bunch lettuce
1 cup chopped celery
1 11-ounce can Mandarin oranges, well drained
A small handful of sliced almonds, browned in butter

THE DRESSING

1/2 teaspoon salt
1/2 teaspoon black pepper
2 tablespoons sugar
2 tablespoons apple cider vinegar
1/4 cup vegetable oil
A dash of Tabasco
1 tablespoon minced parsley

Shake dressing ingredients together in a tightly closed jar. Make up the salad (you'll have enough for six people), pour dressing over it, toss, and top with a sprinkling of almond slices. The crunch is nice, and the flavors work together marvelously.

PÊCHES MELBA

One of Escoffier's best-known dishes was created for Nellie Melba, the reigning operatic soprano of the time. For much of my life, pêches Melba was a sort of Holy Grail to me, although I wasn't an errant knight out looking for it. I just let it haunt me, the way we let things like Truth and Beauty float about shapeless out there somewhere at a great distance.

My father was a singer as well as a preacher, and Nellie Melba was among the pantheon of opera stars whose names came to us, as if from the clouds, in a rich Sicilian baritone liquid with vowels and soft consonants and rolled *r*'s: Caruso, Galli-Curci, Patti, De Luca, Gigli—and not just Italians, but Homer, Chaliapin, McCormack, Melba. I never heard him mention pêches Melba, but he did love Melba toast.

When I got into cooking and adopted Escoffier as my culinary father, temptation came upon me. Try it, a little voice said to me; let's taste this thing called pêches Melba. It wasn't just hanging there on a branch within easy reach; like Faust, I had to go to the books. What I found, of course, was no agreement at all as to what constitutes pêches Melba. One recipe called for canned peaches, others for poached fresh peaches; one called for slivered almonds that others didn't mention; some said raspberry puree, others raspberry syrup, others fresh raspberries.

So, I went to the creator. In *Le Guide Culinaire*, he poaches skinned peaches in a vanilla-flavored syrup, puts them on vanilla ice cream, and coats them with raspberry puree. In *Ma Cuisine*, he sprinkles fresh peaches with sugar, puts them on the vanilla ice cream that seems a constant, covers them with "sweetened" raspberry puree, and adds sliced "green" almonds. Further, I have read that he originally used strawberries instead of raspberries. It's enough to make you want to be damned sure you never call in Truth and Beauty for a closer look.

My way:

Fresh peaches, skinned, halved, and pitted
Raspberry syrup
Vanilla ice cream

The vanilla ice cream should be good stuff, of course, preferably just pure whipping cream with sugar and vanilla—heat 1 cup of the cream until it begins bubbling around the edges, turn off heat, stir in 1 cup of sugar, put in a vanilla bean and leave it in until the cream has cooled. Chill, then add another 3 cups of cream and use whatever device you have for making ice cream at home. This makes a generous quart of ice cream so rich you'll use only a small scoop for each peach half.

The raspberry syrup can be made from frozen raspberries if fresh ones aren't available. Crush the berries and squeeze them in several layers of cheesecloth; stir in two parts of sugar to one of juice. Bring the mixture slowly to a boil; remove immediately from heat; allow to cool.

Some of the new young chefs might put the ice cream and peaches on top of the syrup, but I do it the other way around—not only because I love the colors (raspberry over peach over creamy white) but because I have enough trouble getting food on the table without, as a college friend of mine used to put it, flustrating my mind with all them frivialities—like current fads in presentation.

8

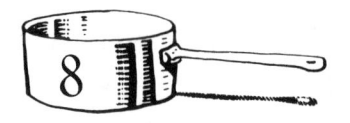

The Pasta Machine

I am as bad about cooking utensils and machinery as I am about cookbooks. Not too long after I'd developed my youthful enthusiasm for cooking (the enthusiasm was youthful, of course; I wasn't), one of the clerks in Overbey's Emporium, the gourmet shop I frequent, suggested that they put up a cot for me. A few months later, another clerk asked, "Was it you who bought that huge copper stockpot we had for so long?" I nodded, trying to keep my self-satisfaction from shining too brightly. "Well," she said, "you are the biggest sucker we get in here. Did you know that?"

Hell, I liked that pot. I still like that pot. It not only sits up on top of the cabinet with lordly authority, it gets used quite a lot, and without it I couldn't make stock and meat glaze nearly as efficiently. My utensils are not just for looks. Several years ago I asked for copper measuring cups for Christmas and got a handsome set that would have done nicely if they hadn't been all off when I checked them for measure. I took them back to the cooking section of the huge department store they had come from and asked if they had any other copper measuring cups I could trade them for. The clerk showed me another set. "What about these?" she asked.

"They're nice looking," I said. "Are they accurate?"

Her eyes got big. "You're going to *use* them?"

I've forgotten how I verified to my satisfaction that these indeed measured quarter, half, three-quarter, and full cups, but I did, and I cooked with them successfully for a long time before I discovered that two half cups did not fill up the cup measure, but two three-quarter cups filled it exactly. That left me with a dilemma. Had I been slighting half cups of ingredients all this time, or had I been putting in too much where one cup was called for?

How to find out? I could check them against the aluminum set I'd had all along, but how would I know that *it* was accurate? I could compare them with my glass liquid measure, but all I've read says that liquid and dry measures are different. And even if I found out what the difference is in fractions or percentages, which measure would I assume was accurate enough to trust? It wouldn't surprise me if both the glass beaker and the copper set were made by the same fiendish perverter of the standard cup. I suppose there is a standard cup, kept along with the standard pound and the standard yard somewhere in Washington, D.C., but I haven't had a chance to go check mine against it.

When I put all this to Candy, she said, "A pint's a pound the whole world 'round."

"That has to be just for water," I told her. "Or milk." My father used to weigh up the fresh milk, and as I recall it, eight pounds was a gallon.

"For anything," she said. "A pint's a pound . . ."

"And maybe oysters." I think they told me that at the meat counter at Brownie's. "But, I mean, a pint of feathers isn't going to weigh the same as a pint of lead, now is it?"

"A pint's a pound the whole world 'round," she said again. "We learned that in school."

I could see that I had to come up with my own solution, which, such as it is, has been to trust the one-cup measure and use the half cup when I feel that a slight half cup is called for, and the three-quarters when it seems as though the recipe needs all it can get, within reason. It seems to work, although whether better or worse than before I discovered the inaccuracy, I can't tell; nor do I know whether it would be better to use my old set of aluminum cups, but they're so cheap and flimsy that I don't intend to find out.

If I can't enjoy cooking, I'd just as soon not do it. And among the things that I enjoy, in addition to copper, are what I have to recognize as intermittent feverish compulsions. When I first got my Cuisinart, I made dishes that not only would have been extremely difficult by hand but would not have been done at all without my mildly insane desire to use the new toy to the hilt.

I remember concocting a special meal for Candy, including fish and seafood quenelles, gnocchi, and a mousse for dessert. The mousse was okay, and the quenelles had a decent flavor, but the meal was not a rousing success because, as I should have known, Candy doesn't like stuff ground up and put back together, and she doesn't relish a plate full of food that looks as if it had all been found under the same rock.

The pasta machine was a greater success. Our friends Terry and Larry came up and gave us a lesson in making pasta, and I got so carried away that I was almost like my Sicilian relatives who used to ask, when you came to their house for the evening meal, "Have you had pasta today?" They may have been checking so that they didn't feed you the same thing you'd had at noon, but I really think they felt that everyone must eat pasta at least once every twenty-four hours.

Since I learned to make it fresh, we've used the store-bought dried kind only when we need special shapes, like shells or little pellets, mostly in clear soups for lunch on cold days and before Candy's indoor soccer games scheduled at times that preclude dinner. The machine I have is one of those that Italy inundated the country with a few years ago. Every gourmet cookware store in this vicinity—and there are several now—put them up front in great stacks of square boxes at roughly half the price they had been, and I'm sure every would-be cook in the United States bought one.

I had images of the manufacturer herding in droves of the unemployed and all their relatives to make pasta machines by the millions in one frantic spate—one machine for every household that subscribed to *Gourmet*, *Food and Wine*, *Cuisine*, and/or *Bon Appétit*—and then when the subscription lists ran out, sending all the workers home with a litre or two of wine to tide them over while a new generation takes its time to develop.

The pasta machine has turned out many a dish for us, of fettuccine, spaghetti, lasagne, cannelloni, and tortellini. The cutting part has only two widths, one for fettuccine and one for spaghetti, but if you press it out to the thinnest setting you can approximate spaghettini, and two settings back from that gives you something like linguine. Wide noodles, like lasagne, are easy enough to cut by hand with a little fluted roller.

I'm not sure why I haven't added to my collection the cutters that do other widths; it seems like something I'd have been compelled to do. Instead I got hung up on the ravioli attachment. "Don't buy it," a graduate student told me. "My sister got one, and she says it's not worth it." Of course, by the time

I'd begun to talk about getting it, there was no turning back; I was hooked already. So, Nonsense, I told myself; her sister is probably not half as skillful as I am with gadgetry.

When the sister of a graduate student issues a warning now, I heed it with a trust bordering on panic. I mixed up a batch of filling I had made ravioli with before, by hand, being sure to get it moist but far from liquid. Then I made a couple of eggs' worth of pasta, kneaded it with the machine until it was nice and elastic, pressed it out to what I judged was the proper thinness, put the ends of two long flats into the ravioli machine, and spooned some stuffing in between. Buono! Now, turn the handle, and out the bottom comes a double row of neatly formed ravioli—except, instead, out came a ragged mass with stuffing not only showing through in some places and falling out from others but all gummed up in the machine.

I said some things, but I cleaned up the mess, thickened the stuffing, and tried again. Same mangled result. By the time I had thickened stuffing and reworked pasta at different thicknesses about eight or ten times, I had used up all my vocabulary and had begun to resemble, both physically and mentally, the soggy stuff my new machine insisted on extruding. Candy begged me to quit, and finally I gave in; but I didn't admit defeat. It must work some way or other, I told myself, or they wouldn't be making the things.

I have forgotten now how many sessions I put in before I called myself beating the machine, and I hope I never remember. What I discovered was that, in order not to gum up the works, the pasta had to be so thick and so heavy with flour that the ravioli had none of the pleasant lightness and delicacy Terry could achieve with considerable ease by hand. Further, at the lengths that I tend to make pasta, I'd end up with half a dozen little ravioli plus a couple of truncated squares leaking their insides out into the rollers. In order to make enough at a roll-through to matter, I had to learn to estimate the wads of dough so that they would come out to exactly the length to make a double row a dozen long, and judge the stuffing so that it came out even.

In all the time I put in, I managed to salvage half a plastic sandwich bag of more or less intact ravioli to hold in the freezer until I should make enough additional for a meal. I never did. After several years of evaporation and freezer burn, those few ravioli rattled like old pecan hulls when I threw them into the garbage.

MAKING PASTA

The way Terry and Larry taught me to make pasta is simplicity itself, and the recipe unforgettable: for 1 egg, use 1 cup of flour, 1 pinch of salt, and 1 teaspoon of olive oil. Make a well in the flour, put in the other ingredients, and work them together with the fingers of one hand, pulling flour in from the sides as needed. Sift leftover flour back into the flour cannister.

When the dough reaches kneading consistency, divide it into one-egg portions (halve it, in other words, if you've made two eggs' worth, and quarter it if you've made four), flour one portion, and cover the other with plastic or wax paper. Run the floured dough through the pasta machine at the widest setting, dust it with flour, and lap it over in thirds, pressing from the near side to the far to prevent bubbles. Run it through again and repeat until it is nice and elastic; then, without folding it, run it through successively smaller settings, flouring as needed, until it reaches the desired thickness—usually the fifth setting on my machine. Hang it over a broom handle or something to dry for a spell (I just lay it out on a cloth on the table).

When it begins to take on a slightly leathery quality, it's ready to cut. It can be somewhat drier for the larger fettuccine setting, but for the finer spaghetti cutters it should be just dry enough not to stick, or it will wad up too much on the sides. If it should begin to wad up, roll it on through if it will go, and you probably won't know the difference when you eat the pasta.

Cook it the way you would dried pasta, only not as long. It should swell up a fair amount, and that's about all; you want it *al dente*, not cooked till it gets soggy or comes apart.

Simple? Of course, like anything, it takes doing a few times to get the hang of it and feel secure about it. And you can do it even a bit more simply, as I most often do now, I confess, to save time. I make it the Terry and Larry way now and then just to keep my hand in, but my daughter, Nina, put me on to letting the Cuisinart mix the dough. Measure into the Cuisinart, fitted with the metal blade, 1½ cups flour (I use the half cup marked "½," not the one marked "¾" that may be a half cup), a pinch of salt, and a tablespoon of olive oil; start it running and break in two eggs. Sometimes that will be sufficient to gather the dough, but if not, add a little water at a time until the dough rolls up on the blade. Let it go around a couple of times, remove, and finish the way you would if you had done it right. If I had plates of pasta done this way and the finger way side by side to taste and compare minutely, I might be able to tell the difference, but I've never tried it.

FETTUCCINE ALFREDO

However you spell the pasta or however the dish is labeled (it appears in some cookbooks as *fettucini all'Alfredo* or even *fettuccine al doppio burro*), it can be *squisito*. Obviously, it was popularized by Alfredo's in Rome. I did have it there once and enjoyed it thoroughly, but I don't remember its exact flavor well enough to be sure which of many recipes comes closest to whatever Alfredo did that day. What I've done is work out my own recipe, which I like to think Alfredo has been able at least to approximate.

For 2 eggs' worth (¾ pound) of fresh fettuccine (see p. 87), or ½ pound dried, cream

4 tablespoons softened butter
About ¼ cup whipping cream

to make a heavy batterlike sauce
Mix into this sauce

½ cup freshly grated Parmigiano
A couple of pinches of white pepper
A couple of grates of nutmeg

Toss with hot, drained fettuccine in a Dutch oven or heavy pot heated to 250 degrees, and serve with more Parmigiano (any dish depending even slightly on the flavor of the Parmigiano should not settle for domestic or simply "imported"—it should demand the real thing, imported from Italy).

One nice accompaniment in season is sliced ripe tomatoes sprinkled with a little salt and pepper and chopped fresh herbs, then drizzled with olive oil. It tastes good with the fettuccine, and it also relieves the total whiteness. Serving on colorful Italian plates helps, too. Plenty for two as a main course.

PASTA IMPRESSIONISTA

I don't remember just what caused me to put together the particular ingredients of this dish a couple of years ago, but we certainly have been glad I did. As usual, the dish is sort of a combination of or variation upon recipes long in existence, and it is probably a result of having had certain things at hand.

The dish is better with fresh herbs, as presented, but I do it all winter with fresh parsley, which is always available, and it is still delicious. It doesn't seem to matter a whole lot just which herbs go into it, as long as they are fresh; I use whatever kinds we get around to putting out each spring in the one tiny plot in our yard that the sun gets to over the trees.

The usual

2 eggs' worth (¾ pound) of fresh pasta (see p. 87), or ½ pound dried

serves the two of us, with usually some left over to freeze and for Candy to have as a light meal before one of her night indoor soccer games.

1 clove garlic, peeled
⅓ cup olive oil
1 rather packed handful of fresh herbs (I've used 1 leaf each of sage and mint, since they are rather strong, plus oregano, marjoram, thyme, fennel, and Italian parsley)
1 or 2 ounces prosciutto, in very thin slices
A handful of shredded Italian Fontina

Heat the garlic in the olive oil until it begins to color, then remove it with a slotted spoon and discard. Chop the herbs. Cut the prosciutto into a sort of julienne, half an inch to an inch long (fold it a couple of times, slice across it, then make a couple of cuts across the other way). The Fontina may not shred very well if it's as soft as the last times I've had it, but it needs to be in small pieces. Danish Fontina or Havarti is good, too, and probably, although I have never tried it, Bel Paese, and who knows what else.

Cook the pasta, drain, and return to the pot. Toss in the warm olive oil and the herbs. Mound onto a platter and cover first with prosciutto and then with cheese. Put under the broiler until the cheese melts.

Frozen leftover pasta should be treated gently, setting aside strands as they thaw. Add a little prosciutto and cheese on top and run under broiler.

The name of the dish comes from the muted colors of the prosciutto, herbs, and pasta that show rather opaquely through the cheese. It reminds us more of Monet than of, say, van Gogh or Gauguin, but we don't sit and admire it long enough for it to get cold.

SPAGHETTI SAN REMO

This pasta—a spin-off from pasta impressionista—takes its name from the San Remo sun-dried tomatoes it features. They are quite expensive, but a quarter pound lasts quite a spell, and they have a better flavor for this combination of ingredients than do others I have tried.

As in the impressionista recipe, use

2 eggs' worth (3/4 pound) of fresh pasta (see p. 87), or 1/2 pound dried

and heat

1 clove garlic, peeled

in

1/3 cup olive oil

until the garlic colors; discard it. Then, add to the oil and cooked pasta

1/4 cup lightly toasted pine nuts
8 or so Italian oil-cured black olives cut in bits off the seed
2 or 3 San Remo sun-dried tomatoes, minced

Continue, using

1 ounce prosciutto, in a fine julienne
A handful of shredded Italian Fontina

as in pasta impressionista. Great rich colors as well as flavors. Enough for three people.

SPAGHETTI CARBONARA

Calvin Trillin wants this to become our traditional Thanksgiving dish instead of turkey; I tend to agree, if only because it is so delicious that you don't have to deal with leftovers, even though it's a hefty dish for two people.

For

2 eggs' worth (3/4 pound) of fresh pasta (see p. 87), or 1/2 pound dried

Mix and hold aside

1 egg, lightly beaten
2 tablespoons half-and-half or whipping cream
A pinch of salt
Lots of freshly ground black pepper
2 tablespoons freshly grated Parmigiano

In a frying pan with

2 teaspoons olive oil

cook until crisp

1/4 pound pancetta, diced

Cook and drain spaghetti, and return it to the pot; toss with egg mixture and pancetta. Turn out onto a heated platter; serve with tomatoes, sliced or in a salad, and bread.

SPAGHETTI BALDUINI

In *A Taste of Rome*, her marvelous book of recipes, history, and fascinating old photographs, Theodora Fitzgibbon mentions a dish named for the maître d' of the Rallye Room. The recipe is a secret, but she tells us the ingredients of the sauce, without giving amounts, and what is tossed in at the last: "very thin strips of deep-fried zucchini . . . so crisp they taste like nuts." I had to try it; the version I came up with may be quite different from the original, but the surprisingly delicate flavors of the sauce and the crunchy zucchini make it very special.

For

2 eggs' worth (¾ pound) of fresh pasta (see p. 89), or ½ pound dried

mix and hold aside

½ cup or a bit more whipping cream
1 small clove garlic, pressed
½ medium very ripe tomato, peeled, seeded, and chopped fine
2 tablespoons pimento, chopped fine

Cut

1 medium-small zucchini

into julienne strips (I use the Cuisinart julienne blade), sprinkle generously with salt, and let drain for half an hour; squeeze as dry as possible in a cloth. While the pasta is cooking, toss the zucchini with

Flour

and immediately (otherwise the flour turns to paste and the zucchini strips to wads) deep fry. Drain the pasta, return it to the still-hot pot, toss it with the cream mixture and with the crisp zucchini, and turn out onto a heated platter—or, as I prefer, hold the zucchini and top the pasta with it. This makes a filling meal, with bread and salad, for a couple of enthusiastic eaters.

RAVIOLI

I won't inflict upon you the recipe I used to try out the ravioli machine; it's a perfectly good one, and it wasn't its fault that it made a mess, but why risk it? This ravioli is a rather mild dish, but with nice flavors, probably better as a side dish than as a main course. A little sautéed ground meat added in would move it up to entrée; that would yield a bit more filling, so you'd need to do more pasta or expect not to come out even. But then, I've never once come out even with ravioli, anyway.

This recipe is designed for two hearty appetites, but there will be enough if a friend should happen in . . .

THE FILLING
Mix together

> 1 pound ricotta
> 2 tablespoons freshly grated Parmigiano
> 8 Italian oil-cured black olives, cut into pieces
> 1 to 2 ounces prosciutto, chopped
> 2 San Remo sun-dried tomatoes, minced
> 1 teaspoon minced fresh herbs

THE PASTA
Roll to thinnest setting on the pasta machine:

> 3 eggs' worth of pasta (see p. 87)

Lay the pasta out in sheets and fill before it dries. On one sheet, put scant teaspoonfuls of filling at intervals of about 2 inches from middle of dollop to middle of dollop. Lay another sheet of pasta over the top of this; press down, eliminating air bubbles, so that the filling is sealed in all around. Cut between and beside with fluted roller, making little square ravioli.

Cook ravioli in

Lots of boiling water

a few at a time; lift out with slotted spoon; place in heated, buttered casserole. Before serving, top with sauce.

THE SAUCE
In

¼ cup butter

sauté

4 tablespoons pine nuts

until beginning to brown. Add and heat

½ roasted red bell pepper (see p. 213)

Serve with more

Freshly grated Parmigiano

If making the ravioli by hand doesn't appeal to you, you're welcome to try my machine. It's out in the garage.

LASAGNE

A while back, our friends Doug and Ceci wanted us to meet a friend of theirs, a retired priest named Father John. We set up an evening and a meal: Ceci would do everything but the main course, and I would bring lasagne. We were having a delightful conversation with Father John until we were called to the table, when he seemed to withdraw into himself. He sat gingerly, holding back from his plate, eyeing it warily. Finally he put a bite into his mouth, chewed cautiously, swallowed, and relaxed with a sigh. "When they told me we were having lasagne . . ." he murmured, and we all knew what he meant. Once a friend asked Candy to dinner that night. "What are you having?" Candy asked. "Spaghetti," the friend replied. "Can you come?" "No," Candy said.

I suppose most of us acquired our conception of spaghetti and lasagne from school cafeterias. This recipe, which I've worked out over the years and continue to change from one making to another, is a far cry from what I remember eating in the basement cafeteria of my grade school. Of course, nobody in Mississippi school cafeterias then had ever heard of lasagne, but the spaghetti was out of a can, and everything we ate was tainted by the smell of the place—a blend of scalded tomato soup and damp concrete.

Try to get that out of your head and remember Father John's reaction; then get these sets of ingredients all ready to put together:

LASAGNE PADRE GIOVANNI

Sauté

1 pound ground chuck

until just brown in

> *2 teaspoons olive oil*

and season with

> *A sprinkling of salt*
> *¼ teaspoon freshly ground black pepper*
> *½ teaspoon dried rosemary*
> *¼ teaspoon dried oregano*

Sauté

> *1 pound good bulk sausage, crumbled*

in its own fat until crisp and season with

> *½ teaspoon freshly ground black pepper*
> *1 teaspoon red pepper flakes*

Cook

> *6 slices bacon*

until crisp, and crumble.
Thaw

> *10-ounce package frozen spinach*

and cook slightly in covered saucepan. Drain, chop, and mix with:

> *A sprinkling of nutmeg*

Slice

> *1 pound mozzarella*

Set out

> *1 pound fresh ricotta*

Also set out

> *1 3¼-ounce can whole black California olives, drained*

Cook

> *2 eggs' worth of fresh pasta cut into lasagne (see p. 87), or 12 store-bought dry lasagne noodles cooked*

in salted water; drain, and toss with

> *olive oil*

to keep the noodles from sticking.

THE SAUCE
In

> *1 teaspoon unsalted butter*
> *1 teaspoon olive oil*

sauté

> *1 small onion, chopped*
> *1 large stalk celery, chopped*
> *½ bell pepper, chopped*

and add

> *Large (28-ounce) can Italian plum tomatoes*
> *1 imported bay leaf*
> *1 clove garlic, peeled*
> *A sprinkle of salt*
> *A few twists of black pepper*

Simmer sauce ingredients, breaking up tomatoes, till thickened; remove garlic and bay leaf. If tomato flavor is sour or sharp, add

> *A touch of sugar*

Layer in a 9 × 15 × 3-inch oiled casserole dish, according to whim.
    But . . . I gave my daughter, Nina, a copy of this recipe, and she told me that she had no trouble with it until she came to "Layer . . . according to whim." It seems that she was, at the moment, whimless. So, here's a sample whim; it's no better than any other, but

maybe it will provide something to react against. The only rules are to finish with mozzarella and sauce, so that you get the comforting bubble on top as well as a little color, and to distribute the ingredients so that they make nice strata, even though when squares are cut and lifted out onto plates they're going to look like blobs, anyway.

I like to start with lasagne noodles, made as thin as my machine will do them, then do something like this:

- add half the spinach, half the ricotta, half the ground beef, and a little sauce;
- top that with noodles, then half the mozzarella, half the sausage, and a little sauce;
- then noodles, half the olives, half the bacon, the rest of the spinach, and a little sauce;
- then noodles, the rest of the sausage, the rest of the ricotta, and a little sauce;
- then noodles, the rest of the ground beef, the rest of the olives, the rest of the bacon, the rest of the mozzarella, and the rest of the sauce.

Did that come out right?

Cook in a 350-degree oven for about forty-five minutes. There's enough here for six people, unless two of them are Candy's nephews.

V

The Days Pass Swiftly

"It was already July 15, then within a day or two it was July 17, and, almost immediately afterwards, July 18."

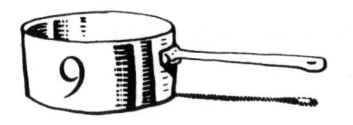

The Back Fence

Our house is angled alongside a circle at the end of the street, so that the backyard is oddly shaped. It is oddly contained, too, with a hurricane fence straight back along the east side and a high wooden stockade fence at an obtuse angle on the west. Connecting the two is a rusted-out pasture fence along a tree line, left over from when this was all farmland.

The old fence was totally inadequate, of course, for keeping in a dog the size of the Bear, as Micawber had come to be called, but he consented to honor the line. Micawber's transformation to the Bear seems to have run parallel to my emergence as a chef of sorts, though if there is a connection, I don't see it. People both here and where we took him to visit family had difficulty with his name. In Memphis he became McCarver, after Tim McCarver, I suppose, Memphis' best-known baseball player. Here, perhaps because we walked him through the cemetery every day, people tended to call him Macabre.

He went through other names, too. One morning, in the vet's waiting room, Candy rechristened him altogether, to save his life. Everybody else there was in greasy-looking jump suits and had a brace of lean, hard hunting dogs. "Whut's that dog's name?" one man asked suspiciously. Candy knew that if she said, "Mr. Micawber," all the hounds would have been loosed upon him in derision, so, inspired, she answered, "Bubba."

Eventually, though, a linguistic variation of his real name is what stuck. Micawber shortened itself to Caw-bear and finally just to Bear, which was what he looked like—big, furry, and without tail—lumbering head on every morning into the tide of children on their way to the grade school just up the street, suffering himself to be admired.

Anyway, if we, like the Bear, had honored the fence line, I would never have teamed up with Marge for that pulpy tomato juice, nor would we have had the further adventures of Dueling Webers, a catered gourmet wok dinner, and the Great American Popoff.

Because of the odd shape of our lot, it backs up both to Marge's backyard and to what used to be Ken and Annie's. Our stepping-over place was established at a low spot between us and Marge, where her husband, Bob, put one of those molded fiberglass chairs on their side to step on, and I found a laminated block of wood for our side. The setup was temporary, of course, but long after my block of wood had disintegrated, that orange chair remained, tilted precariously forward, its wrought-iron feet deep in the ground. It took a lot of traffic.

I recently got around to building the gate that Ken and I used to talk about. It's right at the spot where we used to chat across the back fence, where, in fact, Ken mentioned popcorn one day, and Candy said, "Well, you realize, of course . . ." and Ken said, "I hate to brag, but . . ." and the next thing we knew, the date had been set for the First Annual Great American Popoff, with Candy and Ken as the only competitors. Bob, Marge, Annie, and I were the judges, using scorecards Annie drew up, which involved points for such things as Appearance and Congeniality before the culinary aspects, like Pot Mobility, came into play.

Months before the Second Annual Popoff came around, Ken and Candy began hinting about clandestine preparations for the event. All I knew about Ken's was what I could deduce from arched eyebrows, but of course Candy's I was in on. She had me take her to a tux rental place and ordered up a white set of tails, along with top hat and cane. As the tailor tells me every time I go back there to have a pair of golf pants altered, nowadays they stock such outfits for women—what bizarre competitions other females than Candy may have gotten themselves into, I have no way of imagining—but back then he had to cut down a man's suit and remodel it to fit her. He was so intrigued that we had to take him an official Popoff photo of her in action.

She had practiced pouring with just the right motion of the wrist, too, so that when she broke out glasses and served champagne, the effect was to win her both Appearance *and* Congeniality. Looking back, I sort of regret drawing the line at crystal, but the plastic champagne glasses did travel better, I think, on the drive around the block to Ken and Annie's, and then along the red carpet I unrolled for her.

I was pretty near as dazzled as the tailor was, and until we arrived I felt sorry for poor Ken. I shouldn't have. He was in full Bicentennial brocade, with a tricornered hat and ruffled cuffs. He made a grand little speech of welcome laced with mild clearings of the throat before each self-serving phrase. And he bowed and scraped like an eighteenth-century toady as he took orders for drinks. When I told him, "Martini," he asked, "And what proportions, sir?" So—you feel the need to *test* contestants, if the outcome is to mean anything—I specified eleven and a half to one.

It was a mistake. Because of all the excitement and activity, I didn't realize till later—much later—that what he brought me was not your standard on-the-rocks glass but a tumbler, full. I guess it must have been eleven-and-a-half ounces of gin and one of vermouth. I lasted through the judging fine, though. In fact, we have pictures to prove that I lasted, so to speak, through the recitation of the Corn Creed. There I stand along with the rest, looking as though I were alive.

Ken and Candy were, I have to say, simply elegant, and the effect would have been breathtaking if they could have abandoned for the evening their mutual habit of enjoying their own act as much as, if not more than, anyone else. Candy's suave facade would hold up for nearly a full minute, sometimes, before the observer in her would break through with an appreciative guffaw. Ken maintained throughout the attitude and demeanor of an Age of Reason fop, except for—well, maybe including—an expression with a sappy sort of self-congratulation about it.

As had been the case in Popoff #1, Candy stayed ahead down through Taste and Texture to the final and fatal category: Buttering. She considered herself a purist, and she most definitely was stubborn. She refused to put butter on our Saturday afternoon popcorn, and she would not deign to practice for the competition. Ken, on the other hand, never turned out a batch of popcorn that he didn't butter. His bowl would come out nicely yellow, but still crisp. Candy's—we could always tell whose was whose at this stage—would be sort of half white with soggy patches. Candy rather loudly lamented the fact that Buttering was part of the scoring; "Anyway," she said, "it certainly shouldn't count more than anything else so that Ken can come from behind and win every year no matter how much lead I've built up." But when she tried to claim the Without Butter Championship, Annie made it clear to her that WBC meant *With* Butter, and she was in charge of scorecards.

When Ken and Annie moved away and Candy retired from the ring, I began to take over as corn popper, on a local, amateur basis, of course. I drilled holes in the lid of a thin aluminum pot and learned just when to take it off the flame so the last kernels pop and none is burned. Got a stove-side salt shaker just right for two shakes per batch. I don't want to get something started again, but if Ken had decided to come back the next year and defend his title, I could have been, Buttering aside, a contender.

The Popoff was to be only once a year, but often that first summer the bunch of us would gather around Ken and Annie's picnic table for a feast. Bob would marinate a huge roast and cook it on his rotisserie; Ken would grill ribs on his Weber; Marge would do sweet corn and some kind of potatoes and bring pickles and I don't know what all; Annie would make a cheesy broccoli casserole and freeze up a gallon or so of rich chocolate ice cream full of nuts and things. That was in my precooking days, so Candy and I would haul over little more than a couple of dozen store-bought rolls and our home-grown appetites.

I felt an occasional twinge of guilt until the time Marge volunteered to bring stuffed peppers and later said to Annie, "Why don't you make them? You do them better than I do." Annie lost the right to tease Marge about that, though, a couple of years later, when she and Ken shifted off on me not just one dish but a whole meal—and then claimed it as their own.

By then I had attained a fair amount of skill at the cookstove, of course, for which I have to give Ken some credit. He loved and swore by his Weber grill. I admired it myself and would be almost as brimming with satisfaction as he was the moment he fitted his tongs around a perfectly done thick cut from the tenderloin of some steer. I began, in fact, to believe that a Weber might not be too complicated a bit of machinery for even me. I had cooked on grills before; the Weber added only a lid and a few holes to deal with.

Ken not only encouraged me, he located the first place I ever heard of that sold Webers at less than list price, took me there, and saw to it that I bought one. It wasn't long before our outdoor get-togethers featured what he called Dueling Webers, although he was really in charge of both: side by side, his black one and my red one crowded with ribs. Ken would be hovering about with barbecue sauce and brush, beaming. It shows on my face, too, I'm sure, when I've accomplished something special in the kitchen. It must, or Candy wouldn't say, "You're smirking." But Ken—well, I've always thought of a smug look as fairly passive, but Ken's was like a puddle full of darting minnows.

I learned to adjust the air holes, aim the Weber into the wind, stack fiery coals aside for indirect cooking, and perform all the other complicated moves Ken had already mastered, so that before I realized it I had evolved from caveman, hovering over the suburban equivalent of smoldering sticks and hot stones, to country boy, just itching to take on the bright lights of the kitchen.

The wok Candy gave me as though for Christmas did it. She somehow knew not to give it to me for my birthday the month before; she plucked me up just when I was ripe, and set me down in front of the cookstove with just the right instrument. Standing over that wok was like looking down into the gray eye of the world and *asking* to be mesmerized. It's a wonder I ever put anything in it.

I must have already been reading recipes, because I remember having been appalled by directions like "Stir-fry for fifteen seconds." Fifteen seconds? Even though I could, I was sure, chew gum and walk, if I could stand chewing gum at all, I knew I couldn't count off fifteen seconds and stir-fry at the same time. The timer on the stove would be no help; it wouldn't go off unless you turned it past three minutes, and besides, it would take fifteen seconds for me to get the damn thing set. Such an obstacle might have paralyzed me if I hadn't been determined that Ken and Bob would come to admire me at the range as I had been obliged to admire them at the grill and rotisserie.

So I bought an old-style pocket watch with a little belly-button dial for the second hand and hung it on a hook from the cabinet over the stove. Then I sort of held my nose and jumped in. I think the first recipe I tried was beef and broccoli, on the theory that both *can* be eaten raw, and God knows I had been served them cooked, respectively, to rubber and to mush enough times in my life.

I don't know now why I bothered to hang that watch over the stove. The recipe in the book Candy had with great care chosen to go along with the wok didn't indicate "fifteen seconds"; the basic instruction was "Stir-fry and remove." And it worked. I gave the garlic and salt only a brief bath in the hot oil and put in the flank steak. The thin slices, coated with soy sauce and cornstarch, changed color before my eyes, and, even though I had managed to work up a sweat in those few seconds of concentration, I was able to scrape the beef over the side and put in the broccoli and mushrooms and stock; then I covered the wok and waited for as near four minutes as I could stand. Beef back in, a couple of stirs, and even I could see the cloudy liquid turn translucent and thicken the whole thing into a by-God coherent *dish*.

How Candy divined that I would, I have no idea, but I had an instant affinity for that wok. I could cook with it right off the bat. Maybe because, unlike French cooking, it allowed no time for indecision. With a wok, you don't have time to wonder whether to be or not to be—you do or you don't.

Of course, I invited Ken and Annie and Bob and Marge over the back fence to show off, and I reveled so in the ensuing flattery that before I knew it I had rather grandly consented to cater a dinner, on the sly, for Ken and Annie. They had become entangled in a gourmet club, and their turn to cook was bearing down upon them. They were afraid that grilled steaks, stuffed peppers, cheesy broccoli casseroles, and nut-filled chocolate ice cream weren't exotic enough to qualify, I suppose, and it was like their being, not led, but sort of jerked into temptation when, just in the nick of time and right in their own backyard, a Chinese cook materialized.

The night before their dinner, however, I was struck helpless with a god-awful case of flu. "Tell them," I croaked out finally, " 'You chop, I'll cook.' " I have only the vaguest memory of being held up by Candy, trying not to breathe toward the food, pointing to what I needed, seeing it dumped in— by Ken, I think—and scuffing it about in the wok for the few seconds that seemed, in that timeless twilight of fever, eternal. I have a vague impression of coolies sneaking out the back door with platters of Chinese food, but I think that was either imagination or hallucination. In any case, apparently Ken and Annie got the stuff across the fence, got it served up somehow as though from their kitchen, and, although their debut as gourmet cooks was apparently a success, got themselves out of the club, not only before their turn had a chance to come around again, but also before any deaths caused by flu could be reported.

When I was well enough to sit up and take nourishment, Ken brought me a few barbecued ribs left over from the feast. Until then, I thought I had cooked the whole meal, but the good old Weber had contributed, too, and Ken was justly proud. The ribs were so good, in fact, that I've been doing them ever since. Wok up a beef-with-vegetables dish and another of chicken with walnuts, and then haul in from the grill a batch of Ken's ribs, and you'll pretty near deserve what Bob would comment after nearly every Chinese dinner I tried on him and Marge for as long as he was with us. He'd fold his napkin and say very deliberately, "That's the best meal I ever ate." The tone of that pronouncement carries over in my mind to the one he wrote and signed at the bottom of recipes he prized most: "This I have tried."

Long after Ken and Annie moved away and Bob died, Marge's son, Jim, home for a visit, became the last one to come over the fence by way of Bob's orange chair. On his way back, he stepped safely enough from the concrete block (which I had eventually put down in place of the disintegrated chunk of wood) onto the tilted seat of the chair and to the ground. But then, with some remark about how dangerous that could be when it snowed, he grasped the front of the chair and tried to pull it back up to level. Instead, the whole orange body-fitted shape of fiberglass came off in his hands; the iron legs were still firmly askew in the ground, like a useless quadruple-amputee arachnid.

We both laughed and said things about its being time that old eyesore was removed, and anyhow we had the gate now. But I don't know. It was sort of like watching a last leaf finally give up when you thought you had resigned yourself to winter.

BOB'S ROAST, MODIFIED

Bob used to marinate a rump roast and cook it just so on the rotisserie he had made himself, as he made nearly everything himself. When he saw that the free-standing fireplace we'd had installed before we moved in was too shallow for the length of commercial pokers, he went home and soon came back with a sturdy poker of just the right length, with a wooden handle just perfect to the hand.

He had narrowed the square metal rod down to a proper point at the end, shaped a curled-back piece and welded it on for pulling firewood toward you, and carved the wood by hand. In its place on the bricks that serve as a hearth, it's as satisfying as the nearby painting and the pottery hippopotamus done by other friends, and when we stir up a cloud of sparks with it and watch the flames revive, it's pleasant to think of it as his doing.

What changes I made in the recipe and why, I no longer remember—I couldn't have thought I was improving on the roasts Bob served us. I have steeped rump or eye of round roasts in the marinade I adapted from his for as long as three days; the only times we've been less than happy with the results were when I tried to rush the marination and when I forgot to put in the red wine vinegar. I forgot it again recently but remembered as I was taking the roast out of the marinade and just poured the vinegar over it; that worked fine. Gin in place of bourbon works fine too.

Marinate a roast at least 24 hours, refrigerated, in

1/2 cup soy sauce
1/2 cup bourbon
2 cloves garlic, peeled and crushed

1 small onion, chopped
2 tablespoons red wine vinegar
½ to 1 teaspoon freshly ground black pepper

Drain and pat dry. The roast may be cooked in a 500-degree oven for fifteen minutes, and further at 325 degrees for a total of fifteen to twenty-three minutes per pound, according to taste. Or it can be done on a Weber grill, with a very hot fire and all holes open plus the lid not quite closed for the first fifteen minutes, and then with the lid closed but all holes open. It's great, of course, done on a rotisserie, but I'm not the one to give directions for that.

KEN'S CHINESE BARBECUED RIBS

I think Ken got the recipe from a little booklet, now lost; my apologies along with my gratitude to the unknown author. How Chinese this really is I can't be sure, particularly since both Ken and I do the ribs on Weber grills made in Indiana. But then, Candy remains unmistakably of the American South even though she gets around in a little Italian convertible.

The procedure is simple: Marinate up to five pounds of pork baby back ribs for three or four hours, then cook them over charcoal. With the Weber, I use the indirect method—coals piled up off to the sides, an aluminum-foil pan under the rib rack, and the lid on, all holes open. The meat should not be cooked so long that it dries out, but it sometimes takes close to three hours before it is nearly falling off the bones, which is the way we like it. Bob's rule of thumb for ribs was that they are done when you can easily separate them with your fingers.

The marinade:

½ cup soy sauce
½ cup pineapple juice
½ cup rather dry sherry
1 clove garlic, peeled and crushed
1 medium onion, chopped
1 teaspoon powdered ginger
3 tablespoons brown sugar

The original recipe called for only 2 tablespoons of sherry, but I did it by faulty memory last time, and the ribs were better than ever. The extra sherry may not have been the reason, but why risk it? Also, the instructions allowed for the option of overnight marinating and suggested basting, but either drowns out the taste of the pork.

For hot Chinese mustard, mix some dry mustard with a little vinegar and water and let sit for half an hour. That's great with the ribs, along with plum sauce, which comes in jars or cans from the little Asian grocery where I get gallon cans of Kikkoman soy sauce, and generous jars of hoisin, and sesame oil that's not so refined as to lose the color and flavor of the stuff it's made from. As Richard Petty is quoted as saying, you don't want to get too far above your raising.

ICE CREAM

Several years ago, one of my Christmas presents was, pursuant to strong hints, a hand-turned ice-cream maker with a wooden tub. It was given to me by Candy's parents, Velma and (don't laugh) Fat Daddy. That was Candy's name for him when she was a child, although he wasn't and isn't fat, and it has stuck. Not only with her. Once when she was at Ole Miss some friends told her, "We were in Memphis last weekend, and we tried to call you, but there wasn't any F. D. Barnes in the book."

I resisted calling him that for years, partly because I'm a lot nearer his age than that of his daughter and partly because it sounds sort of, well, stupid. But Velma called him that, or Fat Pop; people he worked with called him that; *everybody* called him that; now, I can't help it, I call him that too.

So, anyway, Velma and Fat Daddy gave me the ice-cream maker. I bought an eighty-pound bag of ice-cream salt, and I began experimenting. Of course, I tried to time it so that there was somebody else around to do most of the turning (after all, I did need to be in the kitchen working on the rest of the meal). Candy was the most usual victim; hence it was no great surprise when, a couple of years ago, my Christmas present from her was one of those Italian jobs that does everything but put the ingredients in. She gave it to me in August.

One thing I discovered is that, for my own taste, ice cream should be basically what it says it is: cream. I have made it with just heavy cream and vanilla, and it is a beautiful thing but so rich that it should be served only with strawberry shortcake or pêches Melba (see p. 81) or something. What compromise I've made with cream is to cut it with half-and-half; a pint of half-and-half to one of whipping cream is still rich, but you can eat a decent serving without feeling overstuffed, and it has that simple, *right* taste. Milk and eggs and such cooked up and frozen make good desserts, but they seem more like frozen custards than ice cream. Uncooked cream has the virtue, too, of being almost no trouble at all.

CHOCOLATE ICE CREAM WITH NUTS

This is not Annie's recipe, which was marvelous, but one done, as Frankie used to sing, My Way. I use cocoa rather than squares of chocolate because I have never been able to melt the squares into dairy products smoothly; the result is always a speckled effect. There is nothing inherently wrong with speckled effects—"Glory be to God for dappled things," as Gerard Manley Hopkins wrote—but it irritates me that apparently other people can get milk or cream to color up smoothly when they want to, and I'm stuck with speckled effects whether I like it or not. And anyway, I don't find any advantage, either in looks or in taste, in squares: They're just cocoa with a lot of extra fat, so they can be molded; to melt them is like reversing an unnecessary step. Take my advice, lazy people, and go with powdered cocoa.

In a pot, mix thoroughly

1 cup sugar
6 tablespoons cocoa

Stir in and heat (but do not boil)

1 pint half-and-half
1 vanilla bean (or substitute 1 teaspoon vanilla later, when cooled)

until you have a smooth mixture. Cool, then chill in freezer or in a bowl set in ice cubes.

Add:

1 pint whipping cream

Mix, put in ice-cream maker, and freeze until not quite hard.

Open freezer and add

1 cup lightly toasted walnuts, chopped

Continue freezing until hard. Most recipes say to harden it even more in your refrigerator freezer, for ease of serving and to let it ripen; that's fine, but I also like it spooned up as soon as you've licked the dasher.

COFFEE ICE CREAM

The variety of delicious things that can with profit be incorporated into cream and frozen is probably infinite; one that works particularly well is coffee, but not using, as do most recipes that I've seen, the dehydrated powder called instant. Well, it is instant; I'm just not sure it's coffee. Some recipes call for the coffee to be brewed first, stronger than usual, but the added water dilutes the cream and tends to make granitalike ice crystals; that's fine for sorbet, but for ice cream I prefer a smoother feel.

Candy's sister-in-law, Martha, suggested this recipe and helped me grope it out. She's the one who said to leave in the pulverized coffee beans; they give the ice cream a pleasant appearance (speckled on purpose is fine) and a nice texture.

In a coffee grinder, pulverize

¼ cup coffee beans (I use the same blend as for morning coffee; see p. 226)

Mix the pulverized coffee in a pot with

¼ cup sugar

Stir in

1 pint half-and-half

Bring to the boiling point (but don't let it boil), stirring.
Stir in until thoroughly dissolved

¾ cup sugar

Pour through a strainer that will remove any larger-than-pinpoint grounds, but leave those that are truly pulverized. Cool.

Add and mix in

1 pint whipping cream
2 teaspoons vanilla

Chill, then freeze in ice-cream maker.

A good vanilla for this, and for many other sweets, can be made by steeping a vanilla bean in a jar of vodka. After a couple of weeks you may take out the bean and use it for something else, if you choose; I leave it in just for the look of it. The flavoring is delicate—a lot better than commercial vanilla for mildly flavored desserts, or for those in which the vanilla should be an elusive undertone. Sylvia, at Overbey's Emporium, also uses various brandies instead of vodka; I haven't tried that yet, but it couldn't be bad.

VI

Antecedents

"On her breast the girl wore a locket in which was enshrined a miniature of her mother, while down her neck inside at the back hung a daguerreotype of her father. She carried a portrait of her grandmother up her sleeve and had pictures of her cousins tucked inside her boot. . . ."

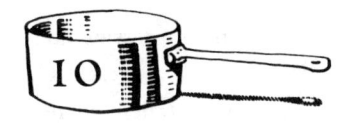

Still Farther Back

I think of Auguste Escoffier as my culinary father. Pierre Franey is sort of an uncle, Craig Claiborne a first cousin, and James Beard out toward the edge of claimable kin. People like the Galloping Gourmet and Chef Tell and Jacques Pepin would be turned away from a family reunion, but Julia Child, well, I can't decide whether she's a favorite aunt or a big sister.

My real family, too, had something to do with my turning out to be a cook when I finally got around to growing up. I may have inherited some of the desire from my father, although he approached the cookstove only once in my memory. My mother was in the hospital, if I recall correctly, and he was left to fix dinner for himself and the four of us. He couldn't call out for pizza or step over to the nearest McDonald's or go pick up a pastrami on rye—if there was a delicatessen in the state of Mississippi, we'd never heard of it, and the byways had yet to be cluttered up with fast-food outlets and pizza parlors. Frozen foods were still in the future, too, so we were spared the chicken pot pies and TV dinners on which a friend of ours recently managed to survive the interim between wives.

My father could have opened a jar of something and warmed it up, I'm sure; my mother canned virtually everything we didn't eat fresh from the garden. And I suspect she had left him some sort of instructions, knowing how helpless he was certain to be. If she did, he ignored them. It was as though he had been waiting all those years for his Big Chance. I don't remember the whole menu, but I do remember his rapt expression as he leafed through a cookbook, and I still have a clear image of the potatoes-on-the-half-shell he proudly brought to the table.

My grandmother, too, must have made some impression on me with her culinary skill, if the family legend is true that, at a very early age, I told her that she was a good cooker. My memory of her kitchen, there in Standing Pine, Mississippi, is of coffee being ground in the iron mill on the wall, thick slabs of bacon sizzling in an iron skillet, and puffy white biscuits coming out of the oven of her wood-burning stove.

In her dining room there was a tall wooden safe with metal panels punched out in some sort of design; through the holes—which looked as though they had been made with hammer and nail—you could smell three kinds of cakes, one of which was always a pound cake, and as many kinds of pies. After we'd eaten our choice of dessert, and after she and my mother had taken the dishes back to the kitchen and washed and dried them, she'd untie her apron and say, "Now, let's go to the house." We'd giggle at "to the house," which must have been a holdover from when kitchens in the old South were separate buildings. Hers was attached, though stuck as far off as possible, beyond the tacked-on dining room. I wonder what she would have thought of my kitchen, which pretty nearly *is* the house.

She mailed me packages of thick, rather unsnappy gingersnaps all through my stint in the Navy during World War II; when they'd reach me in places as far from Standing Pine as the Philippines, their brown-paper wrapping disheveled and greasy, my crew would see to it that they didn't last long. They were always good, but no two batches were alike. "I declare," my grandmother would say about whatever she had cooked, "I don't know why those last ones turned out different. I did them just the same." She might even as she spoke be measuring up flour and baking powder and salt for another batch, by fistfuls and palmloads and pinches.

She didn't grow her own flour and such, of course, but nearly everything else she got directly out of or off of the soil. From her garden she gathered tomatoes, picked okra and pole beans, dug potatoes. Field corn was grist for the mill you could sometimes hear chugging away down the road a piece; when she said "bread," she wasn't talking about a loaf of sliced white stuff in a plastic sleeve ("Pshaw," she'd have said if you'd suggested such a thing; "Be ashamed!"), she meant a slab of cornbread turned out of a black iron skillet. The pigs, in their pen out back in sight of the smokehouse, got mostly slop from the kitchen, but corn helped feed the cows she milked and the hens that turned into Sunday dinner when they stopped laying. Those pound cakes were made with freshly gathered eggs, and with butter she had agitated into being with a long wooden dasher in a stoneware churn.

I recall only two blemishes on my grandmother's record as a good cooker, or rather as a good provider of food. One she couldn't help. There was no preventing cows from grazing on bitterweeds, with which Mississippi pastures grew yellow in summertime. The other resulted from her habit of imprecise measuring, I suppose, unless she just liked her sausage so overpowered with sage that it would pucker your mouth like a green persimmon.

Our cows had the bitterweed problem, too, when I was growing up, but in our small pasture we three boys could pretty well control the crop with sickles. We did so reluctantly; my mother had to flay us with quotations from the Bible and Captain John Smith to get anything done in the garden, too. She could have raised, harvested, and canned the whole crop with the energy it took to set us hoeing around the hills of beans we'd never amount to.

I'm not sure what, if anything, my having to help grow fresh vegetables had to do with my ultimate preoccupation with cooking and eating. I don't cook many vegetables—for our greenery, I often slice avocado quarters and sprinkle them with lemon juice, pepper, and a touch of salt—but that's more Candy's fault than mine. She grew up down South a full generation later than I did but still had to eat green beans cooked so that they tasted like tap water boiled down in an aluminum pan. Say "vegetable" to her and she's liable to shout, "There one is!" the way Marge does when she sees a snake.

I wasn't all that keen on vegetables, either, as kids seem not to have been for quite some time, including the children of some good friends of my parents. Once when they were having dinner with us, and the three kids had obviously been ordered to eat whatever was put before them, Bill, the middle one, asked to be excused for a minute to go out and look at the sun. An odd sort of notion, anybody who didn't know Bill might think; we considered it normal, for him. I suppose it must have been, too, since he grew up to be a meteorologist. Anyway, as he got up, he stuffed his entire helping of spinach into his mouth; when he came back, his cheeks no longer pooched out like a chipmunk's. Later, we came across the wad of unchewed spinach in one of my mother's flower beds.

I was perverse enough to like spinach, but I agreed with Bill and his brother and sister when one of them, speaking for the group, told their mother as she was putting the finishing touches on a birthday dinner, "You've got a meal here fit for a king, if you just don't drag in any old turnip greens." I don't think I ever knew anyone under the age of consent who took to turnip greens willingly; now, though, when I'm in a sufficiently down-home restaurant in the South, the first things I look for are turnip greens on the menu and pepper sauce on the table.

Many things from our garden I remember with pleasure: asparagus shoots smelling of earth from their ferny corner of the garden, tomatoes still hot from the sun, young English peas or butter beans released with a fresh green smell from pods almost tender enough to eat. Nowadays, I could eat my weight in field peas, but I don't recall their being favorites when I was a boy. One afternoon I was working in the garden, reluctantly, I'm sure, when I was stopped dead still by a craving for sweet potatoes, which I had always hated. The craving had diminished by the time they were mature enough to dig, but I didn't balk at sweet potatoes after that, if I could split one open hot from the oven and flood it with butter not too long out of the churn.

We didn't work a long dasher up and down to make butter, the way my grandmother did. Our churn was glass; you set it on the kitchen table, turned a crank, and watched the wooden paddle gather the butter into a formless yellow blob. Now, that was real butter. Some product has been advertising itself on television lately as containing "real *creamery* butter"; to us, much as we might have envied city folk their gussied-up lives, anything not from your own cows or your own hens' nests or your own garden wasn't real, certainly not if it had been pressed into identical rectangles, machine wrapped, boxed four to the pound, and trucked out to grocery stores.

Although lots of non-Sicilian Mississippians had fruit trees, we thought of ours as part of my father's Old Country heritage. From the many-trunked tree beside our garage, we'd fill molasses buckets with figs for my mother to put up as preserves, and for us to eat, cold from the refrigerator, on our breakfast cereal. We would have already eaten all we wanted as we picked, peeling down from the stem to the translucent flesh, the rich flavor enhanced by the smell of fermentation from those the blue jays got to before we did.

We had peaches, too—five trees big enough to climb; we'd dare ourselves out to the ends of limbs for the ripest. We ate peaches prepared every way imaginable; some we merely rubbed the fuzz off of before taking the first bite; others we cut up and froze into ice cream; still others my mother turned into deep-dish pies—simply by cutting them up in a deep pie pan, sprinkling them with sugar, dotting the top with butter, and laying on a crust. Of course, she put batches up for winter, too. One of our family gatherings was on the back porch around tubs of water floating with ripe Elbertas, all of us peeling away, while from the kitchen came the bubble and clink of quart jars being sterilized.

For meat, back in the Depression days of my childhood, we depended mainly on chickens. We did have a pot roast now and then, and spaghetti with meatballs or a meat sauce—a specialty of my mother's, so good that when my father returned to the Old Country he kept telling his Sicilian kinfolk that my mother's spaghetti was the best in the world. Once we had a calf slaughtered, and once a kid, back when we had goats for a spell, but chicken was the staple meat. Nowadays, when I get a chicken the dirty work has already been done: the beheading, the scalding, the plucking, the eviscerating. Most of the preparation fell to my mother, but we ended up with what you don't get now—the complete chicken. Well, except for the head, and we could have kept that if we had wanted to. Escoffier garnished dishes with cocks' combs, but we didn't. The feet, however, were considered essential to chicken soup. My grandmother would gnaw on them with great pleasure, but I'd remember too well what was underfoot in the chicken yard.

"Whole" chickens nowadays have neither heads nor feet, of course, but they have an odd assortment of innards neatly packed in some kind of paper and stuck back inside. They usually have only one neck and one gizzard, but I've often found two livers and sometimes several hearts. In terms of eating, that doesn't bother me; Candy wouldn't touch any of these parts anyway, so I separate out the livers, to cook when she's off on a trip with one of her soccer teams, and freeze whatever else shows up for stock.

But what I don't understand is where the extra parts come from. Are there chickens with three hearts? How are they mounted—parallel, or in series? Or do chicken packers favor those of us who trade at Brownie's Market in Westerville with giblets nature intended for people somewhere else in Ohio? One of these days I'll have to ask John the Butcher, my source of information on everything that goes on behind the meat counter. I've meant to for a long time, but I guess I've been afraid I'd learn something I'd rather not know about the difference in chickens now and when I used to watch my mother reduce them to a standard number of parts.

Unlike most Southern cooks at the time, my mother didn't fry chicken. She learned to do a kind of fricassee—one of the dishes I still look forward to when I go to see her. It's not technically a fricassee; it's simply chicken pieces browned in butter, seasoned with salt and pepper, then covered and simmered over low heat, with a little water if too dry, until very tender. My father was sort of a health faddist, and besides, he had a digestive system that fried foods played havoc with. How he survived as an evangelist I do not know. At most of the rural and small-town churches, he would be housed with one family, who would feed him breakfast, and he would eat dinner and supper at one home after another throughout a revival. There was no such thing as lunch, of course. When an old Mississippi friend invited me to dinner a few years ago, I said, "Now, do you mean lunch? Or do you mean supper?" He snorted. "*Dinner*. At noon. Lunch is something you carry in a paper sack."

The women would load both dinner and supper tables with all their best cooking, and they would be insulted if the preacher and singer (sometimes my father was both) didn't eat heartily. Besides mashed potatoes and sweet potatoes (baked, candied, and whipped with marshmallows on top), snap beans and yellow squash and white squash and corn and okra and butter beans and English peas and field peas, often floating in grease, and besides cornbread and biscuits and rolls—and occasionally, in case the visiting dignitaries turned out to be citified, a plate of light bread—and coffee and iced tea and milk, and three or four different rich and often heavy desserts, there would likely be a ham and a pot roast and, always, chicken.

I kept count when I was with my father at a revival meeting in Hickory, Mississippi, in the mid-thirties, and whatever else was on the table, every single dinner and every supper every noon and every evening for two solid weeks, we had to take our choice of wing or pully-bone (as we called the wishbone) or breast or drumstick or thigh or neck or back from a huge platter of chicken that had been dipped in batter or shaken in seasoned flour or meal and subjected to hot grease. Sometimes it was crisp and delicious; but more often the medium was the message.

Most of the people didn't eat quite like that when company wasn't at hand, but we didn't even if company was. If we had cranked up a batch of fresh peach ice cream, that was it for dessert, or if Mom had made one of her justly famous lemon meringue pies, that was it. We might have several vegetables—not floating in grease—but usually one meat dish, and for starch some of the lightest, most flavorful rolls in the world.

My mother was, and is, a good cook. The prospect of getting home when I was in the Navy conjured up food as well as folks, and those rolls have always been my absolute favorites. I was anticipating them, as ever, on the way home on leave once, from wherever in California I was stationed at the time. Unfortunately, a couple of buddies and I were on a packed train with no service, and as the days wore on we developed a fierce craving for coffee. Although the stop in Omaha was to be very brief, we jumped off the train the instant it quit moving, ran through the large station until we found the USO, and grabbed up cups of coffee as quickly as the ladies could pour them. In the rush, I didn't put a toe in to test the water; I did a belly-flopper. Besides the immediate agony, that coffee scalded my tastebuds to an oblivion that lasted through my entire visit at home. I didn't tell my mother. She cooked every one of my favorite dishes, and I praised them as if I could tell them apart. The rolls I had looked forward to with such anticipation might as well have been cotton batting.

It's a shame that wasn't the time she tried the only recipe I can remember as a failure: Comanche Stew. I think she ran across it in a newspaper, or in some magazine. It *read* good, but it tasted like wet dog.

A dish she made up herself, however, haunted me for some thirty-five years until I ran across its reincarnation. I suspect that my boyhood friend Hugh Albert has as vivid a recollection of the event as I do. He had ridden his bicycle the three miles or so out to spend the day with me. When dinnertime came— at noon, of course—my mother decided to make a batch of spaghetti, which was a favorite "company" meal. When she realized that she didn't have the ingredients for her regular kind, she threw together, in desperation, a sauce made with garlic, tossed it into the spaghetti, and served it with freshly grated Italian cheese. Hugh Albert gagged on the first bite and couldn't go on. But I savored every forkful.

On into middle age I could remember that flavor as though I had just put down my napkin. Ultimately, I asked Mom how she had made it, but perhaps the look of agony on Hugh Albert's face had been too much; the whole affair had blotted itself from her memory. She still doesn't quite believe, although she doesn't put it that way, that I didn't dream up Hugh Albert's visit, bicycle, garlic sauce, and all.

Imagined or not, it stuck in my gustatory memory. So when, during the summer of 1970, probably on a Tuesday, at about eight o'clock in the evening, I sat down for dinner at an Italian restaurant in Provincetown, Massachusetts, and opened the menu to read "Spaghetti con Aglio, Olio, e Limone," I felt like Greer Garson in *Random Harvest* when she thought Ronald Colman was about to remember having been a poor amnesiac living happily with her in a cottage behind a tree covered with white paper flowers. Both Greer Garson and I anticipated correctly, but she got back only a husband and the same old paper blossoms; I was reunited with my beloved garlic spaghetti, garnished now with a nice fresh wedge of lemon.

I was not a cook at the time, but I played around with garlic and olive oil until I could make it, too. It's probably the first successful dish I ever created—if so circuitous an adaptation of my mother's invention deserves that word. Had Candy not liked it, I doubt that we'd ever have begun eating off the same table, but she christened it albino spaghetti and adopted it forthwith. When I'm reduced to asking her late in the day, as I often am, "What are we going to eat tonight?" before she looks up out of whatever she's reading to reply, I know to put the handle in the pasta machine and set a big pot of water on to boil.

MOM'S ROLLS

I have learned to make rolls a good deal like my mother's. Several years ago, I got her to write out the recipe, from which I made rolls that were better than most but nowhere near as good as hers. Later, when she was here on a visit, I got her to show me. Once I saw how thick to make the sponge and watched her method of kneading, I began to peak toward the perfection she long ago achieved—so close, in fact, that I don't dare make them for company if I want people to notice any other part of the meal. Even a very elaborate Escoffier-inspired French dinner went totally unmentioned, once, because I made the mistake of rather incongruously serving Mom's rolls with it.

For someone as absentminded as I am, it's a good idea first to mix and set aside until after the sponge has risen:

A couple of handfuls of flour
1 1/2 teaspoons salt (I use less)
1 teaspoon baking powder
1/2 teaspoon soda

Bring not quite to a boil (remove when bubbles form around the edges)

2 cups milk

Pour into large mixing bowl over

1/2 cup sugar
1/2 cup Crisco

and stir. Let cool (set the bowl in a pan of water if necessary). Meanwhile, in a small bowl, proof

> *1 package dry yeast*
> *A pinch of sugar*

in

> *¼ cup warm water (105–115 degrees)*

Give the yeast time to show you that it intends to rise, then stir into the milk mixture, which must be no hotter than the water the yeast has been proofed in.

Now dump in nearly

> *3 cups flour*

and stir with a wooden spoon, adding additional flour as needed, until all lumps are gone and the sponge is the consistency of cake batter.

Cover bowl with a slightly damp cloth and put in a warm, breezeless place until the dough doubles in volume; punch down, and stir in the flour mixture set aside earlier plus enough flour to thicken to kneading consistency.

Knead, flouring as necessary to keep the dough from sticking, for about ten minutes. The kneading should not be the sort of get-out-all-your-aggressions kind that you might do in making French bread à la Julia Child. Shape the dough into a ball and cradle it in one hand. With the other hand, give a quick, gentle double lift, then a simultaneous fold toward the center and quarter turn. It's hard to describe the motion, but it's almost as if you were hefting it to judge its weight. Once you feel the steady rhythm of lift-lift, fold-turn, lift-lift, fold-turn, the dough will begin to tell you how it wants to be treated. It should end up plump and elastic, with the surface just beginning to develop bubbles that spread open its skin as you knead.

All or part of the dough can be made into rolls now (a good dozen, altogether) and whatever portion you choose to put by can be shaped into a smooth ball, rolled about in an oiled bowl until it gets a coating, covered, and refrigerated until needed. If still warm, it may rise even in the refrigerator. Keep punching it down until it behaves; if it falls on its own, it's beyond resurrection. My mother prefers rolls made within a week; some people like the slightly sour taste they begin to have later. I usually make buns out of whatever dough I haven't used, anytime up to two weeks later.

To make the rolls, pull off a chunk of dough big enough to roll up a little larger than a golf ball, flatten it into a circle, dip into

Melted butter

coating both sides thoroughly (pour any excess butter over the formed rolls—the more the better), fold in half, place on a cookie sheet, and let rise for an hour and a half or so. My mother cooks them rather close together in a flat pan with low sides, like a jelly-roll pan. Bake at 400 degrees until well browned. Butter liberally while hot. Eat.

In one form or another, this recipe has been printed in several local cookbooks, claimed by a number of cooks who got it from my mother. She was given it, under the name of everlasting rolls, by her sister-in-law from Ackerman, Mississippi, in the early thirties. When I served the rolls to our friends Polly and Pep a few years back, Polly went home and searched out the ice-box rolls recipe her Auntie Ann, in Oxford, Mississippi, had written on a card now yellow with age; it was the same.

So, what to call them? "Everlasting" seems a bit exaggerated, and ice boxes are pretty rapidly dying out of memory. I've called them Mom's rolls for so many years that it would be hard for me to change, but those who don't think of my mother as Mom and never knew my Aunt Irma or Polly's Auntie Ann might consider labeling them by the area where, according to what information we have, they originally flourished: North Mississippi. Then in time, perhaps, that geographical designation will become part of the language of gastronomy, along with Tuscany and Provence.

ALBINO SPAGHETTI

"*Faites simple,*" Escoffier said. Well, this dish is simple if ever a dish was. Heat garlic cloves in olive oil, and *Voilà!* There is your sauce. Of course, without a bunch of ingredients to confuse the flavors, the quality of the ingredients is even more important than usual.

This recipe makes enough for Candy and me to pig out. For

8 ounces of dried spaghetti, or two eggs' worth of fresh pasta (see p. 87)

I use

⅓ cup olive oil

I have used extra virgin olive oil from the Chianti Classico area (I like the cloudier of the ones I have tried), which has an aroma when heated that wafts you up among the cherubs painted on the ceiling. I'm not convinced, however, that a good Luccan olive oil at a quarter the price doesn't taste just as good, even though that first whiff isn't *quite* as heavenly.

Heat

4 large, naked cloves garlic

in the olive oil; when they just begin to brown, remove them with a slotted spoon and discard. The oil should be kept warm until the spaghetti is cooked, *al dente*, drained quickly, and returned to the pot from which it and its water have been emptied. Stir in the olive oil.

Serve with

Imported Parmigiano, freshly grated
A wedge of lemon

Candy squeezes her lemon over the whole mound of spaghetti before digging in. I squeeze out a deliberate drop or two on each bit, and I like to keep only slightly ahead of myself with the Parmigiano. The flavors are more acute when just brought together, it seems to me, than when they've sort of melded into each other. Candy doesn't seem to think so, but I'm right and she's wrong.

FIG PRESERVES

Thou shalt not covet thy neighbor's, or mother's, or grandmother's, or great aunt's fig preserves, is what the Ten Commandments should have said if they wanted to get at the heart of covetousness. There are members of the family, close and remote, who never enter my mother's house without their noses twitching, trying to sniff out where the store of fig preserves is kept, especially in the last few years, when the figs have been hit by cold snaps and the supply has dwindled to a few carefully doled-out pint jars. I'd rather be awarded one of those jars than the Congressional Medal of Honor, even though the ceremony is very private; if you get the slightest hint of publicity you'll end up having to share.

I have never tried this recipe with my own hands; since I got interested in cooking I have been too far away at fig-ripening time, alas, and for several years, of course, if I had been there all I could have done was join the blue jays in mourning. But here's the way Mom does it. Her preserves are thicker and sweeter than any others I've eaten, but that thick syrup seems to keep the figs intact and capture and intensify their flavor as weaker syrups can't.

MOM'S FIG PRESERVES

Wash

1 gallon fresh figs, stems on

Make a slit with a sharp knife in the side of each fig.
Soak in

Slightly salty water

for three hours. Rinse thoroughly. Put in a heavy kettle.
Add

6 or 7 cups sugar

Put over slow fire until juices come to a boil and cook down until syrup is real thick. This should give you five or six pints of preserves.

I assumed, when I read the recipe my mother sent me, that the 6 cups of sugar would be for very ripe figs, and as they're less ripe you'd work your way toward 7. But when I called to ask, she said, "No, it's just that I really don't know how much sugar I put in."

POTATOES on the HALF SHELL

I have no idea now what my father did with those potatoes so many years ago, but recently I came up with a version we like.

Bake

6 Idaho potatoes

Scrape out the insides, leaving skins thick enough to hold stuffing, and put the insides into a bowl.

Mix in

2 fresh hot peppers (1 red and 1 green, if available)
¾ to 1 cup Gruyère, shredded
Half-and-half (enough to make smooth)
A sprinkling of salt
Freshly ground black or white pepper, to taste

Fill potato skins with mixture.

Sprinkle on

A little freshly grated Parmigiano

Bake at 400 degrees until browned.

TURNIP GREENS, FIELD PEAS, and CORNBREAD

Up here in Ohio we don't see turnip greens in the stores. Somebody did grow a very tempting row of them last summer in the community gardens, down on the flood plain of Alum Creek, and we walked past them nearly every morning through fall until they were undoubtedly too bitter to warrant risking your mortal soul for. If I had snitched a mess even back when they were tender and green, whoever planted them would have lost nothing, really—the row never looked as if anybody used them at all. But I'd have had to cook them up for me and cook something else for Candy that night; she hasn't grown into turnip greens yet, poor thing.

It occurred to me that, even though Yankeedom and the Ten Commandments had conspired to deprive me of turnip greens so far, one never knew when the North might become enlightened or temptation become too strong. It might pay to be prepared. So I called my mother the other day and asked for her recipe. She did give me directions over the phone, but she confessed later that she'd had to laugh. A *recipe* for turnip greens? You don't have a recipe—you just cook them. Hers, just cooked, are excellent, and here's the way she does it.

TURNIP GREENS

Wash up a mess of greens (a mess means, as I understand it, whatever amount is enough for the number of people who will be eating), put them in a pot with water, cook until the water is reduced considerably, add a big blob of Crisco (most people use bacon or salt pork), and continue cooking until nearly all the liquid is gone. Be careful toward the end not to burn them, but next-door-to-burned gives them the very special flavor that distinguishes most of my mother's vegetables from the general run. For her, none of this half-raw faddishness that has crept across the country from California, even when it comes to green beans.

You can cook green beans the way Mom does turnip greens (only add a small onion and a pod of hot pepper, and use bacon grease—drippings, to fastidious Northerners—instead of Crisco, if you like), or you can barely cook them, whichever suits your taste. I've tried even collards steamed only fifteen or twenty minutes, and they're really good, even left over and cold from the refrigerator, but turnip greens need to be on the fire a long time.

Cooked turnip greens must be doused with pepper sauce at the table, sometimes half a dozen shots for a plateful. A couple of weeks in advance, stuff a bottle with hot green peppers, fill it with vinegar, and let it sit. It's necessary for field peas, too.

FIELD PEAS

These are sometimes known as cow peas, and outside the South seem hardly known at all. Black-eyed peas or purple hulls can be substituted for them, but they're mealier, not as small and delicate. Fortunately for us, our friend Jim (who is from a farm in Indiana and might as well be Southern) has grown some a couple of times and shared them. And Candy's Aunt Rudelle sent a batch back with us from Memphis last summer.

Wash the peas (about a cup per person) and pick them over. Put them in a pot and cover with water; add a chunk of salt pork or a few pieces of raw bacon. Cook slowly for an hour or so until the peas are tender, but not mushy, and the juice is not too watery. A minced hot pepper, a little salt, and a few grinds of black pepper will go well here.

CORNBREAD

Everybody's got his own way. Many Southerners use only white cornmeal—"Yellow corn is for hogs," our friend Tom says—others like the color of yellow better and claim that it is more nutritious, which the figures seem to indicate. Most recipes call for flour as well as meal, but a discerning minority regard the addition of flour as diminishing, if not overly fancifying, the bread. Mom does this real good, too; she calls it egg bread:

Mix well

> *1 cup corn meal*
> *½ teaspoon salt*
> *1½ teaspoons baking powder*
> *¼ teaspoon soda*

Cut in

> *1 tablespoon Crisco*

Stir in

> *1 egg, lightly beaten*
> *½ to ¾ cup buttermilk*

to make a batter.

Heat until quite hot (it can even be smoking a little)

> *1 or 2 tablespoons Crisco*

in a 9-inch iron skillet (preferably, Mom says, a divided one) at 450 degrees; pour in batter; bake till it browns to suit your eye.

For special occasions, cut up a jalapeño pepper, either fresh, canned, or pickled, and stir it into the batter.

GRANDMOMMA'S GINGER SNAPS

I make chocolate chip cookies all the time; Candy couldn't live through many days without her standard three after lunch. And I've made good gingerbread men and a few other kinds of cookies over the years. But the recipe for chocolate chips is on every package of Nestlé's Toll House Morsels, and I've changed it only by using my copper cup marked ¾ to measure when the recipe calls for three-quarters cup each of two colors of sugar, and I think my three-quarter-cup measure is really a half cup. The other recipes I followed closely, and since no problems showed up, I assumed that cookies must be foolproof. I mean, isn't that where kids start out in the kitchen? Improvisation, though, as I soon discovered, brings on unlooked-for results.

When I decided to duplicate the ginger snaps my grandmother used to send me, they had been fading into the past for more than forty years; nevertheless, I retained a moderately clear picture of rather thick, fairly pale, not-real-snappy cookies about two and a half or three inches in diameter. I read through all the ginger snap recipes I could find and chose the one that seemed likeliest, to me, to come out thick and unbrittle; the cookies I got were thin and brittle. I decided that more shortening would move them toward the ideal, but instead it made them hard as rocks. Less molasses was another possibility, but it didn't really change things much. More flour, to give a stiffer dough, seemed at one point the obvious solution; that would make them sit up and hold their thickness. Instead, it made them flatten out and go immediately, when taken from the oven, from thin patties too soft to lie on a rack to hard flat discs that clung to the pan like barnacles.

Finally I asked my mother if she knew anything about her mother's recipe, and it turned out that my sister, Antonina, was way ahead of me; she had in fact come up with a recipe that seemed to her close to what our grandmother used to approximate with her measurement by eye and feel. It makes good cookies, but as I reported to Antonina, they seem much crisper than the ones I remember. She pointed out that on their way from Standing Pine, Mississippi, to the Philippines they may have lost a bit of their initial snap. I suspect she has something there.

I had wanted to give the world a chance to experience something like what I shared with my crewmates near the coffee urns in the chow hall at the airstrip on Mindoro, where we spent the time between forays over what was then French Indochina, but to do that, you may have to make a batch of these, pack them in a shoe box, wrap it with a brown grocery sack, tie it with string, and take it by train to San Francisco and then by slow boat across the Pacific, tossing it about the cabin now and then to simulate the handling of mail.

GRANDMOMMA'S GINGER SNAPS, ANTONINA'S VERSION

Bring to a boil

1 cup cane syrup (see below)
1 cup sugar
1 cup Crisco
½ teaspoon salt

Add

1 cup flour

and cool. Stir in

2 eggs, beaten

then

2 tablespoons soda

dissolved in

> 2 tablespoons vinegar

and

> *Flour, enough to get the right consistency*
> 2 tablespoons ground ginger

Chill and roll. Cut about ¼ inch thick. Bake at 375 degrees until nicely tanned. Cool on a rack. I came out with more than two dozen cookies, but the number depends on the thickness of the roll.

The addition of flour to "the right consistency" reverts to my grandmother's method, all right. I don't know what it is, but when it got there I seemed to recognize it and quit adding flour, and the snaps turned out fine—even though, too, I can't find cane syrup here and had to use molasses.

MOM'S LEMON MERINGUE PIE

This was one of our very favorite desserts when I was a boy, and it was a hit with company, too. Once a visiting preacher—a seminary professor, no less—announced from the pulpit at our church that what he hoped for in the coming revival meeting was another lemon meringue pie like the one he'd had at our house on his last visit. I'm not quite sure that's what the church had in mind when they invited him, but we certainly understood his priorities.

I have tried from time to time over the years to make a pie that stands up to Mom's—that stands up at all, in fact. That's my problem. Most of the ones I've made taste great but run all over the plate, so that you have a wedge of meringue drooping over a wedge of crust in a pool of sticky yellow stuff. When the pie doesn't set, the best thing to do is spoon it out into bowls and call it pudding.

The last time I made the pie, the filling held up better than ever before; I had called my mother after the penultimate time and said, "I cooked it well over ten minutes, and it's just liquid, even after it's been chilled in the refrigerator." Ten minutes is right there in her handwriting in the recipe she sent me. "Oh, I don't time it," she said. "I cook it until you can see the bottom of the pan behind the spoon when you stir it."

So I tried that, and it certainly firmed up more. Nevertheless, after Marge tried the piece Candy took her to the back fence, she called to say, "That's the best flavor I've ever tasted in a lemon meringue pie, even if it is a little runny." Her first suggestion was to use cornstarch instead of flour, but—who knows?—flour may be why the flavor is so good. Her alternate suggestion was to cook it until it gets a sort of sheen, or clarity (I don't remember her exact words), and I'll do that next time if it takes all day. My fear has been that it will be tough and gluey, but I have never come close to error in that direction, I should realize; if I'm going to leave it less than perfect, it might as well be out the other side. Nina says she just cooks it until there is no doubt.

Also, she doesn't use a double boiler; stirring constantly, she says, makes one unnecessary. I like that. I've seldom had much luck with double boilers.

MOM'S LEMON MERINGUE PIE

Combine in the top of a double boiler

½ cup flour
1 ¼ cups sugar
A dash of salt

Add and mix in thoroughly

1 ½ cups water
3 egg yolks

Place over hot water and cook, stirring constantly, until you can see the bottom of the pan behind the spoon, or until the stuff sort of clarifies, or gives you a sheen, or until there is no doubt.
Add

½ cup fresh lemon juice
1 tablespoon grated lemon rind

Cool. Pour into prebaked pie shell.
Beat

3 egg whites

until foamy. Add

¼ teaspoon cream of tartar

Then add

6 tablespoons sugar

2 tablespoons at a time, beating after each addition. When all the sugar is blended in, continue beating until the meringue stands in peaks. Pile lightly on the filling and spread till it seals to the edge of the pie crust all around. Bake at 350 degrees for approximately fifteen minutes; the meringue should color up nicely.

VII

From Humble Beginnings

"... with what trepidation she had overhauled her scant wardrobe in order not to appear unworthy...."

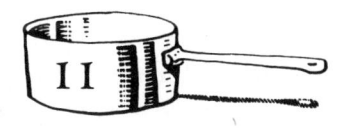

The Shriek of Celery

A lot of people are bothered by recent methods of raising food for the table, with chickens in cages from the time they hatch until they get the hatchet, never having walked around and pecked gravel or seen the sun or run squawking from a rooster. And with cattle not driven like cattle across the plains, but kept in a sort of incubator for their entire span of existence.

Is chicken meat not as good for having been raised clinically rather than having spent its life running and scratching and pecking in a rather foul chicken yard? Is it better to keep an animal that is bred solely to be slaughtered ignorant of beastly pleasures, or should it be allowed a "normal" life until it is killed in its prime?

I begin to lean toward vegetarianism when I think about such things. If I had to do the killing, instead of meeting my chickens already beheaded, defooted, and unfeathered, and my cows already cut into steaks, I might indeed try to exist on barley water alone.

When I was a boy, we often saw chickens go the whole route from living creatures to Sunday dinner. We kept chickens for the eggs, for the flesh, and even for a sort of companionship, in the case of the ones I separated out as pets. I named one set Penrod and Sam, and another Shadrach, Meshach, and Abednego. We didn't eat those. I doubt that we would have even if they had lived to be friers, but in any case a weasel beat us to them, or maybe a large rat.

My memory has my mother killing the chickens that we did eat, and then plucking and eviscerating and cutting them up for a fricassee, but now she tells me that she was never able to do them in. I'm sure that my father sometimes killed one, and my grandmother did when she lived with us. At some point so did I, trying to face the fact, I suppose, that if I were to eat chicken somebody had to force the transition from alive to dead, and why should I be exempt?

I long ago gave up hunting, although it didn't matter to the animals very much, since I was never able to hit either the rabbits or the squirrels I thought I was aiming at. Once I was given a squirrel, though, that someone else had shot. I managed to get the skin off and the guts out, but when it came to the table I couldn't eat it.

Maybe that's part of the reason that nowadays I think of myself as specialized: I do the kitchen work; somebody else gets the meat into the counter up at Brownie's Market. Anyway, even if I could chop a chicken's head off with an ax, as I once did, or still break the neck with a quick jerk, rather than just swinging it around and letting it stretch until the ugly chickling begins to look like a swan, I could never get a chicken plucked. The only time I was involved in a chicken fry that started from scratch, I was assigned to the cleaning contingent. Everybody else had denuded half a dozen carcasses before some kind soul said, "Here," and took over my first and only one, still more than half covered with feathers.

The one pig killing I witnessed I'd just as soon not talk about. I'm not sure why it's more traumatic to see a pig or a cow killed than a chicken. I know that chickens seem stupid by comparison, at least in human terms, but I'm not sure that gives them any less right to live.

And what about vegetables? Plants are alive, and, according to people who have hooked them up with sensitive devices, they show reactions and responses to external stimuli. Which is to say that they seem to feel and maybe even think, and that the fact that they can't run away doesn't mean they aren't afraid, or that they want to end up in soup. I mean, humans are supposed to be bright, and all, and we know that there are sounds beyond our rather limited range of hearing, so why do we seem confident that celery doesn't shriek as it is cut from its roots?

I'm not at all sure that plants don't have personalities. I know that dogs and cats do, and cows do (you should have known placid old Fenwick, or the rambunctious heifer my father named Prettyface), and even chickens named Penrod, and there's an oak tree up in the cemetery, where it has been for more than two centuries, that we speak to every morning. Its presence, and I don't mean just the fact that it's there, seems to require it.

Candy planted some bittersweet out at the front of the breezeway last year, and this spring one of the plants has grown tall enough to go over the edge of the roof. You'd think that's where it would go, feeling its dumb way toward the sun, but this one insists on coming under, into the darkness of the breezeway. Maybe the smells of what we cook on the grill attract it. I don't know how to ask.

We don't know, don't we? as Robert Frost's Job says. And one of the things that I don't know is how to live without eating other living things. I understand that at the Findhorn community in Scotland they apologize to each carrot before they pull it up. I rather like that, but I can't think that it helps the carrot a whole lot. And even if we could go beyond vegetarianism into mineralism, there are microscopic creatures living on everything. Maybe they are too small to matter, to us. I doubt, though, that they are thinking in terms of size as we crunch them with our teeth.

I don't have any answers, and I ask the questions as seldom as possible, but survival and appetite have led me to a practical solution. Margaret Fuller is said to have decided that she accepted the universe. Well, I've decided that I accept its edible parts.

12

That Depression Mentality

I had the privilege of growing up during the Great Depression. It may not sound like much of a privilege, but it was grow up then or not at all, and I not only managed it, I enjoyed it. Furthermore, it has stood me in good stead in later life: Who with more authority than my generation can silence younger people with, "*I* know the value of a dollar"?

Younger people are silent, of course, only because it goes without saying that a dollar is worth what it will buy, and if some of us old fools won't make cornbread until a five-pound sack of meal gets back down to nineteen cents, well, let us eat cake. But we've earned the right to say that we know the value of a dollar, and, good Americans that we are, we may not agree with what we say, but we'll defend to the death our right to say it.

The other lingering advantage I derived from surviving the Great Depression is that, unlike Candy, who has lived through only Minor Recessions, I have a classic excuse for being cheap.

Of course, an excuse for being cheap is something Candy will never have a use for. The fifteen or sixteen pairs of soccer, running, and golf shoes that clutter up Candy's side of the closet, along with sweat shirts and sweat pants and shorts designed specifically for various athletic endeavors, are all of the very best quality, though in various stages of wear. She doesn't drive a mint-condition Jaguar XKE classic only because at a certain point in transactions real money has to change hands. She would be living now on a massive bluegrass spread with dozens of thoroughbred racehorses, in fact, if people with money hadn't taken up all the terrain.

Candy doesn't believe that money should be the criterion; she reckons in human rather than economic terms. If she would enjoy Calumet Farm more than whoever owns it, then why shouldn't she be the one to have it? If she is willing to give her entire kingdom for a horse, and Mr. Galbraith from over the way is willing to give only a portion of his, then why should the bid go to him?

Concepts of the way things ought to be come to her easily; the concept of money, on the other hand, has never tainted her mind. When she visited Italy before we married, she told me, they had this stuff called lire and it just kind of didn't matter what you did with it because it, well, just wasn't worth anything. Like, she'd ask some *gelatiere* how much for a cone of ice cream, and he'd take one look at her and say 25,000 lire, and she'd say, "Hey, is that all?" and give him 50,000 and tell him to keep the change.

"Wait," I couldn't keep from saying, "are you sure you're talking about 50,000 lire? I mean, the exchange was about 620 to a dollar. That's forty bucks for the ice cream and a forty-dollar tip."

"Really? Well, maybe it wasn't 50,000. But it didn't matter, anyway. It was just Monopoly money."

Fortunately, she limits her buying to things she needs and things she wants. I've learned a lot from her. I really have. I mean, even before I met her, if I had gone to the bookstore to get the latest volume by, say, M. F. K. Fisher, I wouldn't have brought home some such thing as *Real Men Don't Eat Quiche* just because it cost less, or figured out to less per word—or because it cost more, for that matter. Money, in such a case, is beside the point. But when I first started to do the cooking and tried frozen vegetables, I would choose a second-rate brand over the best just to save two cents. It took me a while to realize that the beans were stringier, the peas harder, the spinach a less appetizing color. I would go on and eat the stuff not because it was at least marginally nutritious but because You Don't Waste Food.

I would eat it all, in fact; Candy would have hardly touched it. Sometimes I would wake up in the night and go searching for the Alka-Seltzer, without realizing that two of those tablets cost more than the extra I would have paid for something she might have eaten her share of, and without realizing that I hadn't saved a thing by torturing myself with gluttony, no matter how self-righteous I was allowed to feel as *I* cleaned *my* plate, shoveling down the last eight forkfuls on behalf of the starving children in wherever—not a one of whom ever wrote to thank me, by the way, through all the decades that I gorged myself on their account.

Buy only what you want and what you need, Candy began to teach me. If you don't want round steak, which can't be eaten rare, buy porterhouse, or Delmonico, or New York strip. That suited me fine, while I was eating, but at my back I'd always hear a tinny little voice, as from the preelectric phonographs of my early childhood, nagging at me to justify myself.

I decided that probably, if it were really checked out, filet mignon cost no more for the portion that you could eat—since you could eat all of it—than did chuck steak with all its fat and bone. I asked John the Butcher if he didn't think that was the case, and he glanced up from trimming sirloin steaks with his sharp knife and said, "Well . . ." He obviously had not looked into it the way I intended to.

He did the best he could by me, though. He even put an apron on me and let me come behind the meat counter and cut away, measuring my crudely chopped pieces on their professional scales. Our friend Norma took pictures to be published along with my findings.

My intention was to write an article proving my point so as to free up all the housewives who mistakenly feel that they are really saving money by serving only the cheapest of everything. I couldn't, of course, do all the research at Brownie's butcher block, with John trying to work around me every day. That's how I justified my own rather expensive set of scales—they had to be accurate, and I refused to have hundredths of pounds register in my kitchen instead of good old reliable ounces.

I bought pork shoulders and boned and trimmed them, weighed up the skin and bones off chicken breasts, and analyzed blade-cut chuck roast as if I were a forensics expert in a murder trial. I still have cards that read like:

BLADE CUT CHUCK ROAST @ $1.69 lb.

weight 3.46 lb.   price $5.85

meat	1.95 lb.	$56 \frac{1}{3}\%$ = $3.00 per lb. for meat alone
bone	.70 lb.	$20 \frac{1}{4}\%$
fat	.82 lb.	$23 \frac{2}{3}\%$
	3.47 lb.	$100 \frac{1}{4}\%$

This one seems to have been done on Brownie's scales, and I'm not quite sure how I ended up with .01 pounds, or one-fourth of 1 percent, more animal matter than I started out with, but I guess the point was that the edible portion cost $3.00 a pound rather than the $1.69 a pound it may have seemed to the uninitiated to have cost.

This was some time ago, and prices have risen, but, if I remember correctly, filets (I don't seem to have a card on them) cost about $5.99 a pound then. Somehow I began to doubt that I could convince the readers of *Woman's Day* that they would do as well economically to buy filets and forget chuck at half the price.

Candy I didn't need to convince. Her attitude was, eat a half-pound filet instead of a pound of chuck and enjoy it twice as much. I certainly wanted to agree with her. I even asked John from across the counter, "Don't you think filets are *denser*? I mean, chuck seems sort of, well, loose, you know? And tenderloin is very compact."

"Well . . ." John said, and that was good enough for me.

BARBECUE

The reason I fooled around with pork shoulder is that we love barbecue. When we're in Memphis, roughly 30 percent of our intake is barbecue of one kind or other from one place or other. Aunt Rudelle takes us to Gridleys. Fat Daddy takes us to Charley Vergos' Rendezvous. We take ourselves to Three Little Pigs or Topps or Leonard's (where you say things like, "I'll have one Miss White Pig and one Mr. Brown Pig, regular, and one mixed, hot") to pick up barbecued pork sandwiches at lunchtime.

Gridleys' ribs have a wet sauce, and the Rendezvous's are dry, but, like all barbecue I know of in Memphis, they're both pork. I'm afraid that both Candy and I scorned barbecued beef—which as done up here has about the same relationship to real barbecue as forty-nine-cent-special oleo has to real butter—until Irene took us to Sonny Bryan's in Dallas. One taste and you're ready to spend the rest of your life eating off the hood of your car in that parking lot, with suited yuppies eating off their BMWs and men in jeans and boots eating off beat-up pickup trucks, the way it's mostly done at Sonny Bryan's. So far I haven't come close to duplicating his beef barbecue, but I'm working on it.

RIBS

I do my own delicious version of Rendezvous ribs, which is not difficult since, although he won't give out the recipe, Charley Vergos sells the dry stuff to put on them; it's so inexpensive that I haven't bothered trying to figure out what's in it. I use baby back ribs, which are not inexpensive but are tenderer, more uniform, and less fatty than regular ribs, and I cook them by the indirect method in the Weber, using a rib rack, for up to three hours, as I do Ken's Chinese barbecued ribs (see p. 114).

As the unseasoned ribs begin to brown, mop them with a hot water-and-vinegar solution from time to time, enough to keep them from drying out. A few minutes before taking them off, mop them a last time; then as they are put onto a platter give them a moderate sprinkling of Rendezvous Famous Seasoning, available from The Rendezvous, 52 S. Second Street, Memphis, Tennessee 38103.

SANDWICHES

The barbecue for sandwiches is usually pulled (you can ask for chopped) from pork that has been cooked slowly for a long time. It's often called pit barbecue, because the fire used to be built in a pit, which allowed the meat to be at a comfortable cooking level yet far enough above the fire to cook very slowly. Commercially, now, it's mostly done indoors—and privately, many a backyard is blessed with an old steel drum, with the ends cut out, set upright, and topped with hardware cloth or some other improvised grid—but the distance between heat and meat is about the same. In either case, the initial fire is allowed to die down to hot coals before the pork is put on, then additional wood is added every so often to keep it going; flames are doused with water if they get too fierce.

Until I can figure out where in the backyard to dig a pit, I'll use the smoker, which isn't quite right but does remarkably well, allowing nearly twelve inches between coals and pork; with the top on, it tends to keep the heat at a reasonable level. Instead of wood I use charcoal, which keeps itself alive without tending. I do add a chunk of wood at the beginning (most people use hickory, but I generally use sassafras simply because I have it on hand)—enough to give a touch of wood-smoke flavor without smoking the meat as opposed to cooking it.

The cooked meat needs to be very tender. I use pork shoulder, with no seasonings; an 8- or 9-pound shoulder cooks for ten or twelve hours, if just enough coals are used for the fire to be very low toward the end; I just put the shoulder on at night and take it off sometime next morning. The 6-pound one I got last needed to come off sooner, not much over six hours, so I did it in the daytime.

Barbecue sauce is not cooked on; it's added when the meat is put into the bun—along with slaw, unless you ask not to have it; slaw and baked beans are served as side dishes, too. Everybody has his or her own favorite recipe for the sauce, so naturally I do too.

BARBECUE SAUCE

Mix, bring to a boil, and simmer a few minutes

¾ cup white vinegar
1 teaspoon molasses
3 cups Heinz catsup
2 tablespoons chili powder
2 teaspoons dry mustard
2 teaspoons freshly ground black pepper
2 teaspoons Tabasco
¼ teaspoon cinnamon

Take off the heat and stir in

4 tablespoons softened butter

Candy likes it sweeter, and it can go up to equal parts of vinegar and molasses (¾ cup each), but I like it better this way, which is, I admit, a sort of accident. I was planning to try a sauce with somewhat less molasses than vinegar and found that all the molasses I could scrape out of the only jar I had was a teaspoonful. So, what the hell, I thought, and made the radical leap. I haven't been sorry.

SLAW

If you wanted to make Irene get up and leave the room (nobody ever does), all you'd have to do is say, "Spider!" To get the same effect with Candy, say, "Cabbage. Cabbage-cabbage-cabbage!" I'm not overly fond of it either, but I do like a little slaw on my barbecue sandwich, and the best recipe I've found is from the Ladies of Lynchburg. Their recipe box holds index cards I make out for dishes that either turn out well, so that I might want to do them again, or turn out so badly that I want to be sure not to forget and repeat the experience. As I have filled the box up with my own cards, I've moved theirs out. Fortunately, I haven't thrown them away.

One whole section of the cards is about how to do a Tennessee barbecue; the recipe for slaw in it is for hordes of people, so I tried the more modest one in the vegetable section.

MRS. MARY BOBO'S SLAW, MODIFIED

Grate

1 large head of cabbage

Add

⅞ cup sugar

and let stand.

Combine

1 cup vinegar
⅔ cup vegetable oil
2 teaspoons dry mustard

2 tablespoons sugar
2 tablespoons celery seed
1 teaspoon salt

Bring mixture to boil and pour over cabbage while hot. Cover. It will, as Mrs. Bobo says, keep in the refrigerator.

The only things I changed for our tastes and requirements are: the specification of Wesson oil is generalized, the salt is cut in half, and, as is our wont, the sliced raw onion that would stand with the cabbage and sugar is left out. Even Candy says that, for something with cabbage in it, it's good; I mean, since it is just about nothing *but* cabbage, that amounts to high praise.

CANDY'S BAKED BEANS

I was doing barbecue sandwiches and ribs and slaw last Fourth of July, when suddenly I said to Candy, "We're supposed to have beans," a realization at the last possible minute. "Didn't you used to make baked beans?" "I have," she said. I couldn't imagine *why* she had ever baked beans, but there wasn't time to go into that at the moment. "Well, how did you do it?" "Simple," she said.

"Just open

A couple of cans of pork and beans

"Put in

Some catsup
Some mustard
Some brown sugar
Some Worcestershire sauce

and mix it up. And then, on top, put

Some bacon

(Velma slices

1 big onion

on it first), and cook it."

"How *much* catsup?" I said.
She shrugged. "Some. You know, enough to look right."
"And then you . . . bake it?"
She nodded. "In the oven."
"At what temperature?"

She hesitated. I thought I could see figures like 200? 300? 400? going through her head, although they might well have been 6000? 12,000,000? 63? "Till it sort of bubbles up," she said finally. "And the bacon is done."

"I'll try 350," I told her.

So I did. And it was good.

VIII

Coming Through

". . . contrived herself a dress out of a few old newspapers and the inside of an umbrella that would have graced a court."

Waste Not, Want Not

Some years ago I had been driving a visiting poet around, respecting a silence he had lapsed into as the possible gestation period of some immortal lyric, when he finally came out with the fruit of his meditation:

> One thing my wife hasn't learned in
> twenty-five years of marriage
> is to go on and throw
> stuff out
> instead of keeping it in
> the refrigerator till
> it spoils.

Of course the line breaks erased themselves even as he spoke; this was plain old everyday prose, from the heart, surely, but unmolested by the Muse. I wasn't particularly disappointed; I had known the poet for years and had never been in on the birth of one of his poems, unless you count limericks, and besides, as he himself asked on another occasion, how many great poems are written in a century?

If he had, in fact, delivered one of the millions of less-than-great poems a century spawns, I would have been obliged to say, "Hey! Did you just think that up? All by yourself?" or something equally inane and evasive. So I was somewhat relieved at the form of his utterance, but the substance left me feeling a pinch of guilt, a teaspoon or so of defensiveness, and several cups of kinship with his wife, a tall, handsome blonde to whom I bear no resemblance, familial or whatever, outside the interior of our refrigerators.

Since the poet's outburst, I have tried very hard to feed the disposal with what I know in my heart of hearts will never be consumed by humans. But even now, in a search for something on the lower shelves, I come across old olive or pimento jars shoved back into the far reaches; whatever they have been holding for me is long past eating, but upon it, as if to claim for themselves the status of petri dishes, they host isolated cultures of healthy gray mold.

My penchant for trying to save things can be traced, I have to admit, not just to the frugal atmosphere of my childhood but to a book in our home library called *Waste Not, Want Not Stories*. The story that sticks with me as representative is about two cousins, boys of about the same age—the good one, of course, an orphan and the other, having parents, spoiled rotten. The orphan saved pieces of string from packages and what not, rolled them neatly, I'm sure, and kept the wad in his pocket. His spoiled cousin threw away every string that he could get his hands on. So of course they got into an archery contest, each broke his bowstring, and while the spoiled brat pouted in frustration, the good cousin restrung his bow from the wad in his pocket and won the match.

Young people today would have trouble with the story. Where, they would want to know, having grown up with Scotch tape, did they get all that string? Was string the only thing the kid saved, or were his pockets bulging with worn carpet scraps and prickly with old nails? How could used package string hold up against the tension of even a fifty-pound bow, or were they using just whittled-down limbs and sort of looping twigs at targets five or six feet away?

Fie, is what I say to such sophistry. If the youth of today had been trained in Sunday school as I was, the real question would be: Why didn't the orphan, if he was so good, do good to those who persecuted him—give his prodigal cousin a piece of string, and so, as the Bible puts it, heap coals of fire on his head?

The stories in that book did raise all kinds of philosophical, moral, ethical, and spiritual as well as practical questions, none of which kept me from saving string. Nor did the fact that I had neither bow nor arrows, nor that archery contests were as rare in our part of the world as, say, cricket matches. And I saved not only string but everything metal, wood, cloth, or rubber small enough to get into my pockets. My dreams of Want Not glory were less like those of Horatio Alger, however, than like something Walter Mitty might have inspired if I had known him then: The car would break down while we were rushing someone to the hospital, I would imagine, and I would fix it with a rubber band and a burnt-out match stem just long enough to limp up to the emergency entrance.

I have often saved a dozen or two strands of leftover albino spaghetti with much the same sort of fantasy in mind: Craig Claiborne happens in just before dinner (he and I are, after all, both from Mississippi, so why not?) and I scrape together my few strands of pasta, throw in the leftover broccoli with horseradish sauce still sitting in its bowl on the bottom shelf from dinner a week ago, stir in the rice from when friends were here last Tuesday for Chinese barbecued ribs and The Jewels of Mei Tang Poo, strip the four rib bones, survivors of the same meal, and add their pork, throw in the baby limas that Candy wouldn't touch last night, and *voilà!* "Hey!" Craig would say (we'd be on a first-name basis by then), "Did you just think this up? All by yourself?"

Unless Craig shows up within the next few hours, I will have eaten the leftover ribs for lunch, have kept the rice for a while longer hoping to make fried rice to freeze for some hurried future meal, and have run the broccoli and limas down the disposal. It hurts, but sometimes it's best to put old vegetables to sleep instead of letting them hang on and suffer. Meanwhile, although that will have cleared a bit of room in the refrigerator for fresher food, its freezer part and the one in the old refrigerator in the garage are bulging with plastic bags full of chicken bones and skin wadded into weird shapes and frozen hard as rock.

Why throw away broccoli and lima beans and keep the skin and bones of chickens? I'm sure no vegetarians and few carnivores would rally behind me at this point, but there is at least a modicum of method in my madness. For one thing, the broccoli has been there too long for me to feel perfectly safe about it. When in doubt, I've learned to tell myself, throw it out. I mean, it's something we'd have eaten if it had fit into any meal we had during its continued lifetime, but it didn't. Without the horseradish sauce on it, it might have had a better chance, but that kind of flavor doesn't go with just everything. And the lima beans weren't all that good to begin with, as Candy would have been the first to say if she had tried them; why set them out again for her to ignore and for me not to enjoy?

But the inedible parts of chicken, at least those that I trim off when I reduce breasts to nothing but tender meat, have flavor and nutritive value to be extracted and consumed. There is always, in fact, some flesh that clings to the bones, and the knowledge that I can simmer the good out of that and use it in another form makes it possible for me to bone out the breasts with a blithe disregard for the concept of waste. I used to carve around each bone so that every smidgen of meat came off as the one big piece, but although that gave me slightly larger suprêmes de volaille initially, when I'd trimmed off the hard red streak where the keel used to be, and the little gristly section on the big end, and all the fat and membranes, then stripped out the white tendon, I'd not only have taken half the day but also have ended up with no more meat than I now get in five minutes.

The half breasts are great in all kinds of ways: filet mignon poulet (p. 223), of course; cut into bite-sized cubes for various stir-fries; substituted for veal in saltimbocca; made into chicken Cordon Bleu; simply marinated in lime juice for a while, sprinkled with a little salt and pepper, brushed with melted butter, grilled, and served with a wedge of lime; or sliced to make a pocket, rubbed inside with Pommery or Dijon mustard, and filled with a little prosciutto and some kind of cheese within the range from Bel Paese to Gruyère, then salted and peppered and brushed with butter or olive oil and grilled; variations on all the above.

The skin and bones are less versatile until translated into stock or meat glaze, but then they are useful in many and fabulous ways, combining sometimes with the boned breasts to make, for instance, suprêmes de volaille en papillote, which is perhaps Candy's favorite dish in the whole world.

What I do is not exactly according to Hoyle, or to Escoffier or Julia Child, for that matter, but it satisfies the Waste Not urge and results in good eating. When the freezers get too full to put anything else in, I haul down my sixteen-quart and my eight-quart and maybe my six-quart stock pots, put in the frozen chunks of ex-chicken, including necks and gizzards and hearts, along with saved-up steak bones, rib bones, pork roast bones, and pieces of roast that we didn't get around to eating.

Cover each batch with water. Add celery stalks and leaves, carrots, whole onions stuck with cloves, parsley, bay leaves, and black peppercorns. Bring to a boil and simmer, skimming off the stuff that rises to the top; partially cover and keep simmering for quite a long time. An hour may be long enough, but two or three gives the feeling that there's not a vitamin, mineral, or perceptible bit of flavor left to be extracted from the solids.

I dip out and then pour off the liquid, while it is still fairly hot, straining it through a dampened dish towel into containers that will sit in the refrigerators overnight. Off with the hardened fat next morning, and into the appropriate stock pots with the clear juices, to be simmered down until they are rich and full of flavor. Some of this goes into ice-cube trays for use as stock when small amounts are needed (when they're frozen, I dump them into plastic bags and put those into paper sacks—which seems to help prevent freezer burn—labeled with a marker boldly enough for me to identify at a glance). More goes into freezer containers for soups and jellied consommé. The rest spends another several hours reducing slowly to meat glaze, which in turn gets its session in the ice-cube trays.

It takes a lot of time. Just simmering water into stock is not a lot of trouble except for having to dispose of about a bushel of used-up skin and bones. The chicken stuff will go down the disposal, but that takes a while, too, and is messy, particularly since the beef and pork bones have to be separated out, sometimes by feel. But it's often into the second day when that stage is reached, and into the third when it's down to soup level, and into the fourth by the time it has reduced and been strained from pot to smaller pot until it is thick enough to coat the back of a spoon with clear, dark juice-going-jelly. Although it mostly just sits on the stove, you do have to stick around and keep an eye on it.

But, good? When I first made it, I got so excited that I began inventing sauces based upon it, with things like strong coffee and Tabasco sauce in them, or three kinds of liqueurs. Now I mostly throw a cube or two into deglazing juices, if I want them richer, or add one to the liquid for the béchamel in beef bourguignon, or put a cube or two in the liquid beneath a pot roast for a better gravy. That's, of course, in addition to the special times when they go into suprêmes de volaille à la bordelaise or that favorite, suprêmes de volaille en papillote, providing the very special touch that made my mother say, when she had opened up the parchment and whiffed the rising aroma and then took her first bite, "That's the best flavor I nearly ever tasted in my life."

You think that didn't free me up? Was I not from that moment a proven nonwastrel? Since then, even though I still may find an occasional quasi petri dish in the refrigerator, I have once or twice thrown away even pieces of string—short pieces, I grant you—and now if the car breaks down on the way to the hospital, whoever is in dire straits will just have to call a taxi, for all the rubber bands and burnt match stems they'll get from me.

SUPRÊMES de VOLAILLE en PAPILLOTE

Escoffier, in his *Le Guide Culinaire*, gives this recipe in an inch of type on one side of a two-column page. He says, in effect, that all you have to do is sauté the boned and skinned chicken breasts briefly, put them between thick sauce italienne and slices of ham in buttered paper cut in heart shapes, seal by pleating the edges of the paper, and finish cooking in the oven. Simple. Direct. You can almost hear Julia Child adding that a child of eight could do it in, say, half an hour, including oven time.

Of course, you do need to find out what sauce italienne is. You locate it by way of the index and observe that it should be no great problem, since all you do is simmer some ham and duxelles in a demi-glace and add some herbs at the last moment. Back to the index. For duxelles in the Escoffier manner, you chop and squeeze the juice from mushrooms and sauté them dry with onion and shallot. You check out demi-glace and discover that it is a refinement, involving meat glaze (q.v.), of sauce espagnole (q.v.), which takes up considerably more space in the book and mentions several hours of different simmerings before it gets around to "next day," and which in turn grows out of brown roux (q.v.) and brown stock (q.v.), which latter at one point requires "12–15 hours." You've already had to make brown stock, once, which you had to give further long-term simmerings, skimmings, and strainings to turn into the meat glaze for the demi-glace earlier in the recipe, by which I mean, of course, later in the procedure.

Searching backward for what goes into the dish makes you feel as though you're the protagonist of Stephen Leacock's "The Retroactive Existence of Mr. Juggins" (q.v.); then when the process is laid out so that you can contemplate it from first step to last, you get a whole new concept of how a recipe may be handed down from generation to generation.

My method is an adaptation, as you might guess since I do it several times a year. The stock I begin with is what I make from chicken skin and bones; it is a little brown from grilled porterhouse bones and ribs from roasts seared at 500 degrees for their first fifteen or twenty minutes in the oven, but it's hardly what *Le Guide Culinaire* calls for. If Escoffier knew what I have been up to, he would die—if he had not already done so back when I was a culinary innocent of nine, possibly to avoid ever having to face what I was destined to do to his recipe.

What I end up with might be light years away from Escoffier's in taste, texture, and who knows what all, but it's marvelous, and anyway it's as much as I can do and make a living. Maybe when I retire I'll get Irene to come live with us and be co-chef and, with Candy working as sous-chef, I'll use up my golden years doing it just exactly as Escoffier describes it, step by step. If it's any better than mine, I'll be wafted out of this world at just the right time.

I think I'm right in saying that I did my version from scratch once in two hours—that is, from having the stock and meat glaze already on hand. You've got to have the stock and meat glaze on hand. It's worth a lot, too, to provide in advance for an even greater head start. When I make duxelles, I do a big batch and freeze them, so that I can just saw off a chunk when I'm into the en papillote recipe. And I also make sauce espagnole enough for several meals; that cuts the preparation time down to little if any longer than for your average everyday normal meal—a redundancy matched only by my average everyday normal methods in the kitchen.

The sauce espagnole part of the recipe makes enough to freeze some for future use; the remainder of the recipe is set up for four, allowing a whole breast, or two papillotes, per person. We have had guests for whom one was enough, but they invariably saved the other to eat cold the next day.

SUPRÊMES DE VOLAILLE EN PAPILLOTE

VELOUTÉ

Make a roux with

> 6 tablespoons unsalted butter
> 8 tablespoons flour

and stir over low heat until medium brown. Stir in slowly

> 3 cups stock, heated

and cook to a smooth, thick velouté. Hold aside till next step.

SAUCE ESPAGNOLE

> 6 slices of moderately thick bacon, cut into bits
> 3 carrots, chopped
> 2 onions, chopped
> 4 tomatoes, peeled, seeded, and chopped
> 2¼ teaspoons dried thyme
> 2 imported bay leaves
> 1 cup dry white wine
> Velouté from above

Fry the bacon in a heavy saucepan; add the carrots, onion, and tomatoes; brown them a bit; add the thyme and bay leaves and the wine; stir in the velouté and cook down slowly until the mixture begins to thicken.

DEMI-GLACE

> 6 tablespoons meat glaze (see p. 172)
> 1¾ cups of the sauce espagnole
> 4 tablespoons Madeira

Add the meat glaze to the sauce espagnole and cook until a bit thicker; add the Madeira.

SAUCE ITALIENNE

2 tablespoons duxelles
4 ounces cooked ham or prosciutto, chopped
Demi-glace from above
½ teaspoon dried tarragon
½ teaspoon dried chervil
1 teaspoon parsley, minced

Add the duxelles and ham to the demi-glace and simmer until thick but still quite moist. Add the herbs; simmer a moment longer.

SUPRÊMES

4 whole chicken breasts, skinned, boned, and halved
Salt
Freshly ground black pepper
2 tablespoons butter

Season the chicken breasts lightly with salt and pepper and sauté them slowly in the butter until lightly browned and nearly done.

TO GO EN PAPILLOTE

8 thin slices ham or prosciutto
Sautéed chicken breasts, above
Sauce italienne, above
8 pieces of parchment paper, about 10 × 14 inches, cut into heart shapes
Butter

Butter the parchment hearts nearly to the edges. Put the ham slices across the center of each heart, so that they will fold around the chicken breasts. Spread the ham with sauce italienne and lay a half breast on each; fold the parchment and pleat it, beginning at the indentation at the top of the folded heart, overlapping the pleats around the cut edges and giving the pointed end a twist to secure the pleats.

Bake in a 375-degree oven on a cookie sheet until the parchment puffs and begins to brown. Serve as you choose: Either cut an X in the parchment and eat from it, or open the hearts and scrape the contents onto the plate.

Even though neither appears to be native to the France of Escoffier, I prefer Black Forest ham or prosciutto in the demi-glace and slices of prosciutto folded around the suprêmes.

BONING

When I started boning chicken breasts, I looked at all the instructions I could find, including photographs and sketches, and then got John the Butcher to show me how he does it. For some reason, none of the methods seemed totally compatible with my neurological and muscular formation—or perhaps it was my eye and imagination that didn't quite jibe. Anyway, I fiddled around with the chunks of palpable skin and bone and flesh, knife in hand, until I began to find a procedure that suits me. It may fit nobody else in the world, though likely we'll never be sure, because I doubt that anybody will be able to reproduce it from my account here.

John the Butcher leaves the breast whole and leaves the skin on till last to help hold it together; he removes the keel bone and then works from the front of the breast, cutting out the collarbone first and then the rib bones.

That's probably a much better way than (my way):

- Cut the membrane along both sides of the keel bone, scoring around the head of it with your knife; flatten the breast with the heel of your hand, then bend it back until the keel bone is exposed enough to get your fingers around and work free;
- Cut the breast in half along the line where the keel bone was and through the collarbone, unseen but felt;
- An inch or two from the little end of a half breast, stick the knife between flesh and bone, blade outward, and cut the tail of flesh free from the bone;
- Place the half breast bone side down on a cutting board, lift the flap of loosened flesh from the bone, and cut beneath it with a

slicing motion around the bone structure as the flesh is progressively lifted;
- Sever the half collarbone from the rib cage by bending them apart and cutting between;
- Pull off the skin, still attached to the bone;
- Cut out the collarbone;
- Trim away all fat and gristle;
- Hold down the white tendon in the fillet with a thumbnail against the cutting board and scrape the knife along it, blade down, pushing the flesh off the tendon;
- Do the same with the other half breast.

It takes me about five minutes per breast, and I do it best with a heavy French chef sort of knife, very sharp—which I hope John the Butcher never finds out, since he went to the trouble of getting me a professional boning knife for the purpose.

SOUP from STOCK

Sometimes when Candy is puny, or has been ice skating all day in a windchill factor of twenty below, or just gets a craving, I make up her favorite soup. With good rich stock on hand, it's easy. Just thaw a pint in a pan, heat it, toss into a bowl a few thin rounds of raw carrot and half a handful of cooked shell pasta, fill the bowl with hot stock, shake in a few drops of Tabasco, add a teaspoon perhaps of dry sherry, and there it is. That will leave some heated stock, so I generally make myself a bowl, too. If not, it freezes fine all over again.

The variations of this soup are infinite. The flavorings can be changed to suit your mood: less Tabasco, or none, a few drops of Worcestershire sauce; perhaps some bitters. And rice goes well in place of pasta; or neither, if you prefer. Almost any vegetables can be added or substituted for carrots. And there's nothing at all wrong with the stock just by itself, though you may want to season it a bit.

So much for hot soups; the stock makes excellent cold soups, too; just improvise, as I did to come up with

COLD CELERY SOUP

Cook

Chopped celery

in

Stock (see p. 172)

until tender; strain and discard celery.

Add

A sprinkle of white pepper
A few drops of Tabasco

Chill until not quite jelled; garnish with chopped celery leaves; serve. The slight feel of heat from the pepper and Tabasco is very pleasant with the cold of the liquid and the delicacy of the flavor.

IX

Calm Before the Storm

". . . they sat on the verandah and watched the moon sweeping in great circles around the horizon."

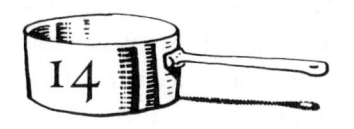

A Cabinet Named Harry

Where I first knew Irene, she and her husband lived in an apartment carved out of the upper part of an old house; it wasn't much bigger than your thumbnail, but she had fixed it up so cleverly that you could seldom negotiate the stairs without stumbling over a photographer from the "Home" section of one or another newspaper in that part of the country.

In addition to the photogenic qualities of the place, I remember particularly a couple of bits of ingenuity: She had made her coffee table of Plexiglas, so that it looked as if it weren't taking up space, then suspended it, so that it could be pulled up near the ceiling when not in use. And she had labeled her kitchen cabinets Tom, Dick, and Harry.

She wasn't just being cute. Her kitchen was often full of college students waiting for her to whip up something good in the few minutes she had between teaching art classes all day and doing sets and costumes and makeup for theater at night; instead of having to stumble over people or shove them aside, she could say, "Hand me the nutmeg from the bottom shelf of Tom," or, "Get the little mixing bowl from Harry."

Irene is and has always been Organized. She hasn't had time not to be, but it's just her nature, too. That's why she used to alphabetize people's herbs and spices. For me, that meant only the minor inconvenience of moving seldom-used herbs to get to the most-used ones, but her blessed rage for order was more upsetting to a friend who had, it turned out, cultivated the sweet disorder in his herbs; eight or nine jars labeled "oregano" may pass unnoticed by mingling, but not when they are cut out of the herd and rounded up.

Except in herb cabinets, Irene has never advocated imposing arbitrary systems of order. She has always been aware that each kitchen must develop its own design; of the three she has set up for herself since the tiny apartment, none has had cabinets labeled Tom, Dick, and Harry, if only because there were more than three to name. And she has been bold to change whatever can be made to work better. Not only did she encourage us to enlarge our kitchen by taking in the entryway, but she was the one who dreamed up the hole in the wall to the living room, and she pointed out that over the sink isn't the most convenient place for an herb cabinet—unless, of course, you need to keep your oregano where it can be dumped down the disposal in case the two guys at the door in plain clothes turn out not to be Mormon missionaries.

So when we had the kitchen done over and the herb cabinet moved across the kitchen to its place near the range, I guess I thought my fumbling days were over. I soon discovered, of course, that crumbling dried leaves into a steaming pot is not the whole story. Since mayonnaise, for instance, has nothing to do with gas burners, I tend to make it over near the sink. That means bringing mustard across the kitchen and, from the herb cabinet, white pepper, cayenne, and paprika, plus eggs and lemon from the refrigerator, corn oil from the cabinet over the range, and the measuring cup from the cabinet beneath it.

Of course, I could make mayonnaise on the cutting board beneath the herbs, but then I'd have to bring the mixer and lemon juicer across the other way, and I'd have to take the eggs across to separate them over the sink. And after I'd gone back across to deposit the yolks in the crock, I'd have to cross to the sink again to rinse my hands, and once more later to rinse off the beaters and the lemon juicer and put them in the dishwasher. I'd have to lie down and rest at the thought of making mayonnaise if the kitchen weren't so small that it's more like a turn than a step from one side to the other.

Over the years I have managed to get things placed pretty well in the kitchen, with help from Candy and suggestions from Irene and Marge. The flatware is handier to the dining room than it used to be (I could swap it to the drawer now full of foil and plastic and have it even closer to the table, but that would move cheese slicer, garlic press, ice-cream scoops, and bread knife farther from the work area); the dishes and glasses are at the dining end of the kitchen, too.

The things I use least are in the small cabinets above the refrigerator, and the step stool I need to reach them is just inside the door to the utility room, which serves, too, as a pantry. Cookbooks are shelved beside and above the utility-room door and over the front door—a bit too high for Candy, but I can reach them, and they are easier to get to than they would be elsewhere in the house.

Still, the kitchen necessitates a lot of wasted motion, and although no one who has waited for me to get a meal on the table would believe it, I have a strong inner craving for absolute efficiency. I have never needed elaborate photographic equipment to do a time-motion study of myself; some little part of my brain is always calculating the shortest distance between two points, whether it's from sink to refrigerator, from knife rack to cutting board, or from plate to mouth.

And counting: it begins counting off the seconds the instant I begin whisking egg whites in the copper bowl for a soufflé, starts again as I combine them with the béchamel and cheese mixture, and yet again when I put the dish into the oven. Of course I don't remember—never even notice, in fact—what the count is for any given action. If I did, I suppose I'd have to write it down somewhere and do something with it.

Ineffective as it may be, my desire to be absolutely efficient keeps me trying to dream up a kitchen that fits that description. What would it be? A circle about six feet in diameter, so that you could stand on a sort of lazy Susan and reach everything without effort? Or what? While I'm waiting to come up with it, I continue to do odds and ends at random, and for impure reasons.

Like sentiment. I recently built a mobile cutting board out of a chunk of butcher block, not because I thought I needed it, but because my son gave it to me and because it came from the kitchen of the restaurant where my friends and I used to go on dates when I was a seventeen-year-old college freshman—Primos on Capitol Street in Jackson, Mississippi. Beneath the mounted block I left an open shelf—with room for my recipe cards, some tins of tea, a stack of cooking magazines, and a yellow Le Creuset pot—above a cabinet filled with stacks of cotton and linen drying cloths. I put the whole thing on casters so that it can be moved across the tile floor almost with the touch of a finger.

It has turned out, in fact, to be very useful in all sorts of ways. One of them might be, it occurs to me now, that I could make mayonnaise on it without all that twisting and turning; load it up with the stuff from the refrigerator side of the kitchen, wheel it across near the sink, and turn on the beaters. I guess I'll have to use up the batch I just made before I can try it, but just the idea is excuse enough to call Irene tonight.

MAYONNAISE

I shudder now to think of slathering "salad dressing" on slices of white bread to make a sandwich, but that's what some of my friends did after school when I was a boy. I may have been envious of their store-bought way of life, but I think I shuddered at least a little even then. I'm not sure what commercial salad dressing was or is, but it served as a cheaper version of mayonnaise and came in the same kind of jar.

Our mayonnaise came in a crock with a wide, blue line around it near the top; my mother made it with beaters somewhat like those on electric mixers, only turned by hand. In summer, we lived on tomato sandwiches and cold chocolate milk, or could have. The chocolate syrup was homemade, the milk was fresh from our own cows, the tomatoes were fresh from the garden, and with that fresh mayonnaise on it, even ready-sliced white bread seemed right out of the oven.

Candy's mother, Velma, still has one of those crocks; they seem to have been part of some promotional scheme for Wesson oil back during the thirties. But Velma seldom uses it; she holds off for the couple of times a year we're in Memphis and lets me do it. When I've finished, she shows up, spoon in hand, to taste and adjust, mostly adding lemon juice, until the mayonnaise is so delicious right by itself that she could stand there and eat the whole crock—which is why she doesn't make it when nobody is there to stop her.

I found a shorter crock that reminds me of my mother's, just wide enough to fit the electric beaters and deep enough to hold a making of mayonnaise. Until I located it, I made mayonnaise in the Cuisinart, but the crock lets it go directly to the refrigerator without changing containers.

It's awkward to hold my little mixer with my right hand and try to control the drip and flow of oil with my left, particularly since that keeps me at a distance that is just wrong for my trifocals, but I have designs on a mixer that stands on its own, and kneads dough, too, if I can figure out where to put it.

Most of the time I have no problem with mayonnaise, but now and then it either stays liquid or begins to stiffen and then comes apart. If it never thickens at all, the only thing I've found to do is pour it out of the crock, put an additional egg yolk in its place, and start over, adding the runny stuff and then the rest of the oil. If it starts to come apart, sometimes adding cold lemon juice will save it; sometimes, though, it won't, nor will dollops of cold water. I read the other day that hot water is the thing, but the only time I tried it, it didn't work.

Weather may have something to do with it. One hot, humid summer I had a long spell of trying to make mayonnaise with no success at all; no matter how many times I started over all I got was thin yellow liquid. That was here in Ohio. Down in south Mississippi, my daughter-in-law, Becky, went through the same thing at the same time, and so did Irene, over in Dallas. Maybe everybody in the world did, but didn't think it necessary to let me know.

I'm not sure how this recipe for mayonnaise evolved; I like other people's just as well, but we've been happy with it, and until just the other day I seemed to have settled upon it. To make about a cup and a half of mayonnaise, I'd beat together in the little crock

2 egg yolks
About ½ teaspoon dry mustard
A pinch or two of white pepper
A pinch of cayenne
A pinch of sweet paprika
About 1 tablespoon corn oil

I'd usually set the mixer on the middle of its three settings, but I never could keep from fooling around with it. When the yolks and stuff were mixed well, I'd begin adding

10 ounces corn oil

slowly; a tiny stream seemed to be best. As the mayonnaise thickened, I'd increase the flow of oil (who doesn't?); if I failed to pour faster, the mayonnaise would either get too wadded up to take the remaining oil, in which case I'd add lemon juice, or start coming apart, in which case I'd panic. Usually I would wait until the end to mix in

Juice of ½ lemon

and I'd seldom taste and adjust. I'm not as finicky about it as Velma is; we don't eat mayonnaise out of the crock, but usually with sandwiches or in pimento cheese. If it was to be used with fish, though, or if I'd been sold mostly rind and seeds, I would squeeze the whole lemon and use as much of the juice as seemed fitting.

All that is in the past tense only because I'm trying something different. Not what our friend Monica tells me is the real way to make mayonnaise—the way her mother makes it—starting with an egg yolk in a cup and mixing slowly with the end of a knife, adding one tiny drop of oil and mixing thoroughly before adding another. I believe Monica; her mother is the most marvelously French person I have ever met, or even imagined. She has to be right about anything associated with *la cuisine* or *l'amour*. But if making mayonnaise had to be that tedious, I'd put it off until the couple of times a year Velma is up here and get her to do it.

What I'm trying now is based on Pierre Franey's recipe for sauce tartare, in *More Sixty-Minute Gourmet*, which is not only absolutely delicious (without the onion, and probably with), but is also an oil-into-egg mixture that has not yet failed to work for me. I've always made the sauce tartare with a whisk, but when I tried that with mayonnaise it remained the consistency of tap water. Of course I shouted to the heavens, "You see! And I did them exactly the same!" After I calmed down a bit, though, and studied the two recipes for a month or so, I was able to discern a subtle difference that probably would have continued to elude minds less keen than my own.

Franey's recipe mixes the egg yolk with, not dry, but prepared Dijon mustard. So I started with only the two egg yolks and about half a teaspoon of Dijon in the crock. I did use the electric mixer instead of the whisk, but the stuff thickened as if it thought it had to, and, after I'd stirred in the lemon juice and the seasonings, it came out just the consistency that I like.

That's once, though, and I've had results as good many times my old way. It's got to prove itself in all kinds of weather, while sun spots are acting up and seismographs are edgy, and, of course, at the time of the full moon, before I'll be able to start pouring oil without my vocal apparatus set to say, "You see!"

YOLKS and WHITES

They don't make egg shells the way they used to. Try as I might to get a clean, even break, when I separated eggs in their shells, at least one yolk in half a dozen would be punctured by a sharp edge. Eventually my mother sent me an ingenious little cup that was supposed to hold the yolk in the middle and let the white run out slots around the sides, but it acted like something designed by Mr. Wizard to demonstrate surface tension. Not a single egg white could I induce to part from its yellow through those slots.

When the movie *Who's Killing the Great Chefs of Europe?* came on television, I felt obliged, as a sort of professional courtesy, to watch it. "Pay attention," Candy said. "You'll learn how to separate eggs." She must be psychic. There it was, demonstrated before my very eyes, so simple that I couldn't believe I hadn't thought of it myself.

When I tried it the first time, I'm sure I experienced a distant echo of the thrill felt by whatever long-ago cook first discovered hands. Sticky as the operation is, straining an egg through the fingers results in a separated egg, and nearly always an unbroken yolk. Just in case, though, I still drop any whites I plan to use into a little bowl one at a time, just to be sure a feebly membraned yellow doesn't mar the purity of the whites and retard their ability to whip into a proper froth.

I used to save extra whites so that I'd have that additional one most soufflé recipes call for, or to use along with cornstarch and what not in pre-stir-fry marinades, or, I'd tell myself, to make meringues some day. But they'd soon turn cloudy in little jars in the refrigerator, and when frozen in ice-cube trays they'd nearly always dry to a nice satiny pith on top before I could get around to using them, or at least to sealing them in plastic bags. So now I am profligate of egg whites; down the drain they go if they can't promise some immediate use.

Yolks are a different matter; when they're left over, I put them in a little jar, and nearly always I'll be making mayonnaise or béarnaise or even hollandaise before long, and I get to feel righteous and frugal as the shiny little yellow blobs slide nicely out of the jar into the crock or the Cuisinart or the double boiler. Of course, if they don't slide, I don't try to force them.

SOUFFLÉS

I think it was Craig Claiborne whose recipe I started from to develop the soufflés we ate every Sunday night for years. With the first few I was apprehensive, but when despite all I could do not a single soufflé visibly bit the dust, I began not only to whisk with a flourish but also to scorn the written word and let memory and a sort of Pavlovian conditioning have their unerring, quasi-instinctive control.

Well, nearly unerring. But accidentally leaving out the salt was a positive error, since the flavors that came through unmasked led me to reduce the salt from then on by two-thirds. So was forgetting the extra egg white; we discovered thereby that we prefer a slightly richer soufflé to a slightly puffier one.

From another error, though, the only thing I learned was, Don't do that. It occurred to me that something could possibly be wrong as I was putting into the oven a much shallower mixture than usual, with a consistency something like that of wet concrete; fortunately, I hesitated long enough to realize that I'd left out the milk. My trained culinary instinct warned against sloshing liquid on at this stage, so I made a thin béchamel that did mix in, after a fashion, but even though the soufflé didn't fall, it didn't rise much, either, and its flavor was as heavy as its body.

When I first started making soufflés, I had real trouble with the cooking time. Nearly every recipe I read suggested some thirty-five minutes, but when I would remove a thirty-five-minute soufflé from the oven and try to serve it, instead of a light and airy section lifted intact from the dish, my spatula would come up with a little flap of crust dripping gooey innards. I'd curse the recipe and put the soufflé back in the oven, where it would miraculously scar over and continue to cook. It was some time before it got through to me that a soufflé is not supposed to be the consistency of a foam-rubber mattress; it needs to be somewhat runny when served, to keep its rich, moist quality and flavor, especially since it continues to stiffen up on the plate.

There are all kinds of soufflés, but Candy has a strong preference for cheese; there are many kinds of cheese soufflés—I've used Gruyère, or Gruyère with blue, or Parmigiano, for instance, with excellent results—but Candy wants them made with cheddar 99.44 percent of the time.

For us two rather hearty eaters:

CHEESE SOUFFLÉ

6 large eggs, separated
4 1/2 tablespoons unsalted butter
4 1/2 tablespoons flour
1 1/2 cups milk, warmed
2 or 3 ounces sharp cheddar, shredded
1/2 teaspoon salt
A couple of good pinches of white pepper

Whisk the egg yolks for a moment in a large bowl. Make a béchamel with the butter, flour, and milk (melt butter, add flour and stir until smooth, pour in milk a third or so at a time, whisking until smooth and a bit thickened). Remove from heat and stir in the cheese, salt, and white pepper. Mix into the egg yolks, a little at a time at first. Beat the egg whites until they form rounded peaks; stir about two-thirds into the cheese mixture, then fold in the rest. Pour into a buttered and floured soufflé dish and place in a cold oven. Turn the oven on, to 350 degrees, and check from about twenty minutes on to see that the top is browning nicely.

The recipe is easily varied. As the spirit moves, I add, along with the salt and white pepper, pinches of cayenne or a few drops of Tabasco, or maybe a half teaspoon of Worcestershire, or some paprika, or some lemon zest, or a little mustard of some kind, or a tiny pinch of curry, or all of the above. Chopped-up roasted red bell peppers (see p. 213) or pimentos are delicious, too, and the colors are nice.

I like the feel of a wooden spoon in stirring the béchamel and for the rest of the mixing and folding; I also rather enjoy whisking the egg whites in a copper bowl, but I doubt that anybody eating the soufflé would appreciate that I had spurned the electric mixer, which may whip them fully as well.

I'm not convinced, either, that it's best to start the soufflé in a cold oven. But how could anyone resist Monica Sheridan's dictum on the matter in *The Art of Irish Cooking*? A savory soufflé, she says, "should rise gradually, like a careful government servant, consolidating its position on the way up."

How to determine when the soufflé is done? There is always the bamboo skewer test, but by the time the skewer comes out clean, the soufflé is drier than we like it. Just as good a test, for me, is the shade of brown—not pale, but nowhere near the burnt stage—and the inner motion of the soufflé as evident from the top: It should lose some of its liquid motion but just begin to firm up.

Most recipes call for paper or foil collars around the top of the dish, to make the soufflé stand up high, I gather, and add to its presentation before it's cut into, but they've never done anything for me, and since Irene says they've never done anything for her either, I've quit worrying about them.

I haven't found a good way to serve a rather runny soufflé. I use a couple of spatulas and then, if necessary, spoon up the rest. It doesn't make a neat wedge, but nothing much I handle does.

With such a cheese soufflé we usually have either sliced avocados with lemon juice, salt, and pepper, or a green salad, or sliced fresh tomatoes.

QUICHE IRENE

Quiches add to the tasty blend of eggs and cheese the texture and flavor of pie crust, and they will accommodate other ingredients that would sink to the bottom of a soufflé. One of Irene's creations is especially good.
Prebake

Pie crust

in quiche dish.
Shred

4 ounces Swiss cheese

Sauté

6 medium-sized mushrooms, sliced

in

2 teaspoons butter

Steam

A handful of broccoli florets, al dente

Toast in pan on range top

¼ cup sliced almonds

in

1 ½ tablespoons butter

Mix well

2 eggs
1 cup whipping cream
A few grates of nutmeg
¼ teaspoon salt
A pinch of cayenne

Fill pie crust in this order: First put in the cheese, then the broccoli, then the mushrooms and almonds, then the custard mixture. Bake at 350 degrees for going on three-quarters of an hour, until the top browns up and the custard is set. The traditional knife-in-the-center-comes-out-clean test seems to be fairly reliable.

AUGUSTA NATIONAL QUICHE

This is not sanctioned by the Masters golf tournament, but that's what we were watching on television when I decided that if Irene could make up quiches, I could too.

Saute

1 small onion, sliced thin

in

1 teaspoon bacon grease

Heat in a covered pot

1 package frozen spinach

until thawed and warmed through. Drain, press dry, and chop fine. Spread sautéed onion slices over the bottom of

Prebaked pie crust

in a quiche dish. Add

4 slices bacon, fried crisp and crumbled
⅓ of the chopped spinach
A generous sprinkling of freshly grated Parmigiano

Beat together

4 eggs
1 cup whipping cream
A few grates of nutmeg
A pinch of salt

A couple of twists of freshly ground black pepper
The remaining chopped spinach

and pour into pie crust.

Top with pennant-shaped cutouts of:

Pimento or roasted red bell pepper (see p. 213)

Talk about presentation! That green with the golf flags is probably as close as I'll ever come to the extravagances of the Carême era. Or, for that matter, to the culinary equivalent of the ceramic "collectibles" that clutter flea markets nowadays.

X

The Plot Thickens

"... at lunch alone with her he struck her savagely across the face with a sausage."

Others, Lord Yes, Others

I may have been a little overconfident in declaring that Candy would never say "my kitchen." She got along suspiciously well when I took over her couch last winter and she took over the preparation of food.

At first I watched with amused tolerance the way her hand would jerk away the instant it had stuck a potato into the oven or clanked a pan onto the range. The rectangular hole in the wall might have been a wide screen, and she Doris Day playing a Russian duchess in disguise as a scullery maid.

Within three days she had cooked everything she had ever tried before except Rock Cornish game hens with pine nut stuffing; it was time for me to get off the couch and, with a superior smile playing at the corners of my mouth, take over again.

That little scheme is pretty well conceded as this year's Best Laid of Mice and Men; nothing, not even emanating from the White House, has gang so radically a-gley. I had interpreted Maurie's diagnosis of "within an inch . . ." as about an inch *short* ". . . of pneumonia"; apparently he had meant that I was out the other side, and his "couple of days in bed" was not a prescription but a prediction of how long I had and where I would spend it.

By the time I had been flat on my back for six weeks, Candy was clattering around like an old pro, improvising not only elaborate dishes but whole menus. I ate each meal with good appetite, perhaps because each one might possibly be my last; but then came the suspicion, nay, the realization, that

Candy and my kitchen were having far too good a time: If I leave them together much longer, I told myself, it won't matter whether I live or die. I got well.

Candy bowed out like the good sport she is; soccer season was coming up soon, and if she did the cooking she might have had to miss practice for one or two, if not all three, of the teams she regularly plays on. She had, nevertheless, developed an understandable fondness for culinary activity and has since become a very helpful sous-chef, even occasionally volunteering from the shallows of some article on Pete Rose or Joe Montana, though never from the depths of Herbert Warren Wind on golf, to wash the spinach for a salad.

I usually let her. I even allow her—as long as she recognizes the fact that it's my kitchen—to come in and put water on to boil for pasta without written permission. I went so far recently, in fact, as to turn over to her the pressing *and cooking* of tortillas while I chopped chilies for a salsa verde and went on to peel and mash avocados for guacamole with only a glance now and then over my shoulder to see that she wasn't flattening her fingers in the Tortilladora.

The truth is, as it wouldn't have been a while back, I enjoy having her there, even though where we both are, there will our Old English sheepdog be also, taking up most of the footroom. When Irene was here last, all four of us would be crammed into the kitchen at once, the upright ones doing a little you-move-here-and-I'll-move-there minuet, and I found even that, in the current jargon, nonthreatening. In fact, what used to be called fun.

For a long time Irene was the only person I willingly let into my kitchen. Not only did she teach me most of what I know, but it was she who introduced me, in the deepest sense, to the kitchen. If the kitchen and I had formalized our relationship, Irene would have been matron of honor. And she has hands that *do* things. Once Candy and I happened upon a magazine with pictures of some actors being costumed or made up, or something, and we both said, "Irene!" because the disembodied hands doing it were so unmistakably hers. Hands like that you'd better turn loose in your kitchen whenever you're lucky enough to have them around.

Of course, when Irene leaves, it takes a week or two to find the garlic press and the wooden spatula, and to get the cooking forks separated from the eating forks. If she just wouldn't leave, everything would be perfect, but the fact is that, in your kitchen, nobody but you knows just where things go. Or even what things are: a while back, one helpful person cleaned up for us after coffee and threw the gold mesh filter into the garbage along with the grounds.

Well, it's the thought that counts, people keep saying; but the deed is what's outside their heads doing the damage. I have had guests plop back in their chairs with that air of, "Well, you can't say I haven't done *my* bit," after I've first begged and then ordered them not to put the dishes in the sink, and then had to sit helpless, unwilling to tackle them bodily, while they bustled about and did it anyway. Far be it from me to question such people's altruism, but I can't help thinking of the Robert Frost character who could never resist the temptation to do right when she could hurt someone by doing it.

I don't *want* the dishes in the sink. They fit down over the drain, and water builds up until it's like looking down into my grandmother's slop bucket, only she could take that out and empty it into the pig trough. No, my helpers go home and leave me to grope for the plates through a film of grease and among bloated chunks of uneaten food.

Helpers of that ilk are the reason I don't offer to help when I'm at other people's houses. It's not laziness, or that I wouldn't like to be of real use, or anything. It's that, in my ignorance of both mine hosts and their kitchens, I might be making things worse instead of better. So I just sit with the rest of the guests and drink and talk and have a good time, confident that if it's the thought that counts in my place, it must be the thought that counts in theirs.

MEXICAN FOOD

Every couple of weeks or so we haul out the Tortilladora, and Candy gets down the little iron skillet that serves as a *comal*. I mix a batch of tortillas in the Cuisinart and thaw the shredded beef I've already prepared for the evening, pour a little Mazola into the larger black iron skillet, and crisp up the beef for mochomos. Guacamole is a regular accompaniment, and salsa verde plus chili sauces made from dried peppers. If we have company, I usually make some gazpacho, too, according to the recipe Irene and I worked out after consulting batches of them in various cookbooks. Also, I do a *nieve*, or sorbet, of lime or tangerine. Since the beef folded in tortillas is finger food, we use paper plates that nobody is likely to stack in the sink whether I protest or not.

My bible for such food, from which I deviate to suit myself, just like all good believers, is Sue Style's *Larousse Mexican Cookbook*, which is the most usable and reliable of the Mexican cookbooks I own or have looked into, at least at my stage of development. I vary her recipes principally by leaving out onion and by using some parsley when I can't get fresh cilantro.

GAZPACHO

We—Irene and Candy and I—like a little texture to our gazpacho, so we add unblended chopped stuff at the end. And Irene insists that the final direction is "Chill-chill-chill." Well, next to final. She is very much into presentation in food as well as clothing, makeup, rooms, houses, and the world in general, so she also says, "Garnish with *parsley*," and she's the one who took notes. I'm not sure why she underscored parsley.

Purée in food processor or blender

> *1 large (28-ounce) can Italian plum tomatoes*
> *1 stalk celery*
> *½ bell pepper*
> *½ cucumber*
> *1 clove garlic, peeled and crushed*
> *3 tablespoons olive oil*
> *3 tablespoons lemon juice*

Add and mix in

> *Tomato juice to thin (about 1 cup)*
> *2 or 3 dashes Tabasco*
> *1 dash Worcestershire sauce*
> *A dash of salt*
> *A few grinds of freshly ground black pepper*

Also add and mix in

> *Other ½ cucumber, chopped*
> *Other ½ bell pepper, chopped*
> *½ fresh tomato, chopped*

Reprise: Chill-chill-chill. Garnish with *parsley*. Serves six.

CHILI SAUCES

My method of dealing with dried chilies was given to me along with two huge bags of dried New Mexican peppers, a few years ago, by one of my students from that part of the country. Debra said to rinse the peppers, put them in water along with some garlic and a little oregano, and cook them until they swelled back up good. Then, drained, they go into the Cuisinart to be pureed, and then through the food mill (large holes) to get rid of the seeds and any unpulverized skins. I don't remember where I got the rest of the procedure, but I sometimes add vinegar, then cook down the puree in a little Crisco or lard until it acts

the way dough does when it pulls away from the sides of a bowl—
that is, it becomes a coherent mass instead of merely a mixture.

The procedure works with all varieties of dried chilies, and we like to play two or more sauces against each other with whatever dish. Anchos are my favorites for this, partly because they are mild enough for you to taste their fine flavor along with that of the mochomos. Some arbols I tried once burned so fiercely that you not only couldn't taste the salsa, but couldn't taste, smell, or feel the meat and tortillas. I did up some cascabels a couple of years ago that were somewhere between the anchos and arbols in heat and had a marvelous flavor; our friend Larry finished off the jar at one sitting. The last cascabels Irene brought from Dallas look totally different, though, and I am wary of them.

The finished sauce goes into a jar that in turn goes into the freezer, to be thawed, dipped into, and refrozen until all used up.

SALSA VERDE

The little Mexican green tomatoes, or tomatillos, that this recipe calls for are usually available fresh here; canned tomatillos are supposed to be acceptable, but since I haven't found them in our markets, I have been forced a couple of times to use the substitute Sue Style suggests: gooseberries. They do make an acceptable sauce, but it is not quite as tart, and since all the gooseberries around here are canned, its texture is a bit limp.

In a saucepan, cover with water and simmer

¾ pound fresh tomatillos, hulled and rinsed
2 fresh green mildly hot chilies
1 clove garlic, peeled
A handful of cilantro
A pinch of salt

until the skin of the tomatillos is beginning to split. Let cool; drain; purée in a food processor. This makes enough for about three meals for Candy and me; it freezes well.

GUACAMOLE

For the two of us, one avocado makes enough to eat with mochomos plus enough for me to have an extra few spoonfuls in the kitchen when Candy isn't looking.

For the consistency we like, I use a potato masher on the avocado and quit mashing while it's still lumpy.

In a bowl, mash

1 ripe avocado, peeled, of course, and seeded

Add

1 small clove garlic, pressed
1 small fresh green mildly hot chili, minced
Juice of ½ lime
Some cilantro leaves, chopped

Stir together gently (you don't want the avocado to lose all texture), put the avocado seed on top (it may or may not help keep the guacamole from darkening, but it does look good), and let sit a while before eating.

MOCHOMOS

FLOUR TORTILLAS

Unless we're rushed, I do a whole recipe of my version of Sue Style's *Tortillas de harina* in the Cuisinart, Candy presses and cooks them, and we freeze enough leftover tortillas for at least another meal. They warm back up nicely in a hot skillet.

Mix in a Cuisinart with metal blade

4 cups unbleached flour
½ cup Crisco or lard
1 scant teaspoon salt

Add, with motor running

1 cup hot tap water

The dough should be pliable but not sticky. For each tortilla, roll into a ball a walnut-sized piece of dough and press it thin in a Tortilladora, or roll it out as thin as possible. Flop it into a smoking-hot ungreased cast-iron skillet, let it begin to brown on one side, turn with a metal spatula, let it cook on the other side until the raw-dough look is gone, and remove. Stack, and cover with a dish towel.

SHREDDED BEEF

The meat for mochomos takes a little doing. I cook a 4-pound or so chuck roast over a whole afternoon, let it cool in the cooking liquid, remove, refrigerate overnight, shred with my fingers the next day (or the next, or, sometimes, the next), and freeze until we're ready for it, when I thaw just enough for one meal.

Simmer in water to cover

4 pounds or so chuck roast
1 small onion, peeled
1 clove garlic, peeled
1 or 1 ½ teaspoons salt

until meat is pretty much falling apart. Cool in cooking liquid; drain and shred. (Freeze what you're not going to eat right away.)

For two mildly gluttonous people, cook about half the beef in

2 tablespoons oil

until crisp.

Fold into tortillas (three each, for Candy and me) and serve with chili sauces, salsa verde, and guacamole. I spread the sauces on the meat and eat the guacamole on the side (I like it in with the meat, but it squishes right out). Candy folds just the meat in, then dips the mochomo into sauces she wants before each bite. There is probably some psychological explanation of our role reversal here as related to the way we eat albino spaghetti, but I don't want to hear it.

MEXICAN RICE

We don't have this with mochomos, since the tortillas provide the starch, but we like it with many other Mexican and non-Mexican dishes—it's really mock-Mexican anyway. The recipe makes enough for four, but I like it left over and either reheated or at room temperature.

Melt in a pot

1 tablespoon bacon grease

Add

1 ½ cups brown rice

and stir till coated with melted grease.

Add and stir as mixture heats to a boil

½ cup tomato sauce (your own) or 2 tablespoons tomato paste in ½ cup water
1 ¾ cups water

Cover; lower heat; cook forty-five minutes; take off heat; let stand ten minutes.

While the rice cooks, char under the broiler

1 small red bell pepper (or use ½ large)
1 small green bell pepper (or ½ large)
1 fresh jalapeño pepper
1 large clove garlic, unpeeled

Peel each under running water; seed peppers and chop; mince garlic; stir into rice with

1 tablespoon fresh cilantro, chopped

Reheat and serve.

NOPALES

Or nopalitos. These are cactus leaves, from the prickly pear, that have been showing up in the supermarkets here for the past several months. I wouldn't have known what to do with them if Becky, my daughter-in-law, hadn't shown me, but they're not difficult to deal with, done my way, and they are delicious.

My way: Get Becky to remove the little spines with the tip of a sharp knife. Cut the nopales into ½-inch squares (you'll need a good handful per person, as you would green beans), simmer in water for twenty minutes, drain, and heat further in the pan to dry them somewhat. Add minced fresh hot pepper and cut-up tomato. Serve as you would any green vegetable.

After a Mexican meal, the light clean taste of a citrus sorbet, or *nieve*, seems just right. This one grew out of a Waste Not, Want Not impulse a few years ago related to a Chinese dish. I had peeled half a dozen or so tangerines, scraped out the bitter white inside, and dried the peel to use, a little at a time, in a tangerine-peel chicken stir-fry we particularly enjoy. There sat the residue: six unclothed tangerines. I might eat one a day at most, but I knew that, with my memory, some month or two later I'd find a plastic bag full of a soggy mass that represented at least four of them. So, I laboriously got the juice out of them (even with the skin on it's difficult, since the skin simply slides off when you turn a half tangerine on the simple juicer I have), made a syrup of it, added the juice of a piece of fresh ginger, and tried it over vanilla ice cream. It made a delicate, very tasty dessert. Why not, I thought when I got my electric ice-cream maker, translate that into its own ice? This is the refreshing sorbet I came up with:

TANGERINE SORBET

Bring to a boil and simmer for five minutes

1 cup water
1 ½ cups sugar

Add

Zest of 3 limes
Strips of peel of 1 tangerine (pith scraped out)

and let cool; strain.
Add

Juice of 3 tangerines
Juice of 3 limes

to equal 1 cup juice, plus

1 cup water

Freeze in ice-cream maker. Store in freezer until hard—a quart container may be not quite large enough.

This version gives a nice granitalike texture; if you prefer a smoother, perhaps even lighter, sorbet, stir in a beaten egg white as you put the mixture into your ice-cream maker.

If you don't have an ice-cream maker, the sorbet will work fine frozen in an ice-cube tray until not too hard, broken up and whirled about in a food processor (add the egg white here, if it's wanted) until frothy, and returned to the freezer in the tray. That's the way I did sorbets until Candy's Christmas present in August took all the work out of it.

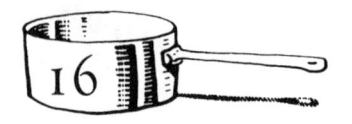

"Did I Catch You at a Bad Time?"

We eat dinner at a civilized hour, most evenings. A while back, when Maurie was in the hospital for some tests, he told a nurse in my presence that once they came to dinner and I didn't put the steaks on until midnight. Midnight, for Maurie, when it comes to dinner, arrives no later than 7:56, but I'm sure he was confusing a steak night with the dreadful hollandaise episode, since which I've made every effort to have food on the table and everybody seated with napkin in lap by 8:00 at the latest.

I do try, but the fact is, we normally eat, whether company is here or not, anywhere from 8:30 to 10:00. Well, not "anywhere from," exactly. Whatever it is in me that makes me count off seconds as I work and makes me want to take right angles when I walk across campus also makes me uncomfortable if I don't serve dinner on the hour or the half hour. So, really, it's *at* 8:30 or 9:00 or 9:30 or, in rare cases—mostly if Candy is playing indoor soccer at night—10:00, with slippage allowed for, as nearly as possible, in five-minute increments.

Nearly everybody else in the world—by which I mean, of course, around here—seems to eat at an hour suitable only for small children who must be in bed, read to, and asleep by 6:30. After they eat whatever it is people eat at that hour, they pick their teeth while they watch the news on television, and then get so bored by some game show that they ring me up on the telephone.

I don't know how many meals have been thrown out of whack in the past few months just by students, former students, and other fellow would-be writers who call at the wrong time. Even the simplest of dinners requires some attention and some timing, and often I don't even have the potatoes scrubbed, dried, rubbed with olive oil, and in the oven before my callers are ready to settle in for a long evening's chat. But suppose I'm past that and have the grill set up in hopes of searing a couple of steaks before the potatoes turn to mush.

"Did I catch you at a bad time?" they say.

"Well, I'll have to get the electric starter out of the charcoal in a minute or two . . ."

"Okay, I won't hold you. Just one question."

Of course, the question takes eight minutes of background explanation. Long before I can begin to make out the rising inflection of interrogation approaching in the distance, I've had to interrupt: "Hang on just a second. I've got to get the starter . . ."

"I won't keep you. But the last rejection slip I got from them . . ."

"Uh, Candy?" I say over the lowered mouthpiece. "Could you get the . . . ?"

"What's that?" my caller says. "I can't make out what you're saying."

Candy, off on her couch, won't have been disturbed from whatever she's reading. I raise my voice: "Candy! Hey, Candy! Would you . . . ?"

My caller's voice rises proportionately: "Well, anyway, they had written 'Sorry' across the bottom. Do you think that means anything?"

Candy has lifted her head. I motion toward the screen door beyond which is the smoking grill. It smells as though every wire in the house has shorted and we're going up in flame at any moment. Candy sniffs. "Oh," she says, and gets to her feet.

"Are you still there?" my caller says. "Did we get cut off?"

"Oh. No. I just had to . . . the charcoal starter . . . what were you saying?"

"'Sorry,' on a rejection slip. Does it mean anything, do you think?"

"Probably that they're sorry they can't accept the piece. But," I can't help going on, "of course they may be commenting on its quality, ha ha."

Writers come in two categories, neither of which stops talking at this point. One despairs immediately: "That's what I was afraid of. Do you think I ought to quit trying?" The other never despairs: "Well, should I send the piece back for another reading?"

Whichever, I ought to say, "Yes, by all means," and hang up; why should I, in the latter case, try to protect some editor who never bought anything of mine, or, in the former, do the suicide prevention squad out of a prime case? But I'm always too weak not to say no in one form or another, even knowing that I'll have to go on and justify it until the coals and our prospects for good thick grilled porterhouse steaks have reduced to a vague pyramid of white ashes. It's too late to eat that heavily by now, anyway, so the only thing to substitute is the only thing that I can do fast enough and that is light enough to sleep with: omelettes, again.

Aspiring writers do have some claim on my sympathy, and I even understand why they call me up despite the fact that I can't answer their questions, and that even if I could, it wouldn't be much help; it's just that they need *somebody* to talk to. I mean, what they're going through has none of the gratification I get in cooking for Candy. She does let me know—and she is nothing if not clear and emphatic—what she won't eat for dinner tonight, but she also helps decide what the menu is actually to be. She even collaborates with me on recipes. And she eats with a gusto that I get to observe, and comments along the way about how good it all is, and heaps on praise at the conclusion of the meal and sometimes off and on for days, if the ribs, for instance, have been lifted from the Weber at just the right moment, as they were the other night.

For writers trying to publish, it's like having to cook in a closed-off kitchen, ignorant of what sort of being with what kind of tastebuds will probably not even bother to sit down to the finished meal, which they have to seal in a manila envelope, drop through a slot at the post office, and let cool and congeal all the way to New York—only to get it back a couple of months later, apparently untouched, with a little printed note saying, in effect, you are merely one of so many whose food we don't like that we've had these printed up by the tens of thousands. If I had to cook like that, I'd be calling up Irene or Polly or Monica—anybody I knew who had had at least one dish visibly appreciated—to say, "I think there was a faint coffee stain on the napkin this time. Do you suppose that means anything?"

But it's not just people I'm even vaguely acquainted with, or people with an interest that comes within light-years of mine, who call as I'm trying to cook dinner. Most of the time it's a complete stranger with no last name who calls up out of the blue—or out of the black, I suppose, at that time of night—to ask me how my day has been:

"Hel-*lo*! May I speak to Mr. Can . . . uh . . . zer . . . oni?"

"Close enough," I say.

"Hi, this is Vickie, with Time-Life Books in Chicago? How was your day today?"

I may not be able to help would-be writers much, but you would-be cooks out there trying to get dinner on the table, let me give you some good solid advice: Don't tell her.

It really doesn't bother me that telephone voices can't pronounce my name. It's that they call at all. It's worse than junk mail. And I should know. Our overladen postperson told me the other day that people who deliver the mail have reason to be aware of who gets lots of mail, and we get *lots of mail*.

It's Irene's fault. She started giving us *Gourmet* quite a few years ago, in the name of Bob and Candy Canzoneri, and they must have sold the list to other publications, who sold the list to developing resort areas that are always holding one of six prizes you've already won, who sold the list to catalogs, so that we have reached the depths of being addressed as Bob-Candy, BobCandy, Bob C., Mr. B. Candy, Bob A. Candy, and God knows what all, and the list has gone step by step downward to seedier and seedier places. Now we get catalogs featuring ceramic Doberman salt and pepper shakers that play "I Did It My Way," and devices to put in your toilet so that when guests lower themselves onto the seat a voice says things like, "It sure is getting dark down here."

As Anna Russell says in her account of Wagner's Ring cycle, I'm not making this up, you know. Our postperson went on to tell about a man who deliberately got himself on every mailing list in the country, and he got so much paper every day that he used one of those log-rolling devices a couple of pages over from the singing Dobermans and heated his house free all winter. But the point is, as awful and as irritating as junk mail is, it doesn't force itself upon you while you're trying to bone out chicken breasts.

We long ago quit answering the phone once we settle down to eat, and we've debated whether we should just quit altogether, even though we do get calls from people we want to talk to, along with those from Olan Mills Studios and people who waterproof basements and will be in our neighborhood on Wednesday. An experience I had the other night, too, has given us pause. Anna Russell and I are not making this up, either, although I hardly expect to be believed. I answered the phone with my usual trepidation, and sure enough, a voice said, "Hel-lo. This is Vickie from Whatchacallit Enterprises. Did I catch you in the middle of something important?"

"As a matter of fact," I said, "yes." Fixing dinner, of course.

"Well," Vickie said, "You go right back to what you were doing. Bye!" And hung up.

Candy was off at soccer practice, and the only thing I could think of to do was call up somebody and demand, "What does this mean? Could it be a sign that there's yet hope for the world?"

OMELETTES

"Omelettes again" may sound disappointing, but only when your taste buds have been tuned to porterhouse steaks. Omelettes are great in their own right, a little heavy for our conception of breakfast but splendid for brunch or supper. We have them at least every couple of weeks, partly because they range from relatively quick to almost instantaneous, partly because at their simplest they are very light, and partly because they are delicious.

Partly, too, because they are very easy to do. A child of eight should have much less trouble with an omelette than with hollandaise sauce in a blender. Nevertheless, an omelette my friend Jan made for me many years ago filled me not only with pleasure—and with eggs and (I think) leftover asparagus tips—but also with awe.

"How do you *do* it?" I asked him.

"It's easy," he said, and he told me how. After I had failed a few convincing times, I got him to *show* me, but still, as a child of, I suppose, forty-two, I was unable to grasp the principle. That was before I learned to regulate heat, and I suspect that was my problem. When Monica went through her Mummy's omelette with me step by step, one of the things she made me do was bend over and look under the pan at the flame as I adjusted it. Since then, omelettes and I have been on fairly intimate terms.

When I have time, I do either Monica omelettes or layered omelettes or frittatas. In a hurry, I do the ones I learned from watching Julia Child on television. I think she timed them out at about twenty seconds each, so I probably don't take over a minute and a half. That's cooking time, of course, though setting them up is also fast and easy unless you want elaborate fillings. She tells all about them, and the layered omelettes, in *From Julia Child's Kitchen*, so I'll talk only about the others.

For a Monica omelette, beat the eggs with a fork, after a little water has been added, just until they begin to combine. Put a good pat of butter into the omelette pan over moderately high heat. As the butter melts, it should be swirled over the bottom and sides of the pan; when its bubbles begin to subside, whip the eggs eight times with the fork, with large lifting strokes five or six inches above the bowl, then pour them into the butter when it first begins to color.

The bottom and sides of the omelette will begin to cook at once; the heat should be turned quite low, and the cooked sides of the omelette pulled inward with the fork or a spatula, allowing the liquid in the center to flow out to the sides of the pan. As the top part begins to firm up, add salt and pepper, along with grated cheese or sautéed mushrooms, if desired, and fold the far edge of the omelette back over to make a half-moon shape. It should slide nicely onto a plate, and it should be tender and moist with not a touch of brown.

As for frittatas, or *frittate*, if we want to stick to the Italian, they are essentially eggs in an oven-going skillet that are cooked first over direct heat until they begin to firm up and then transferred to a medium oven to cook just until the moist look is gone. I use a little water to bind them and beat them with a fork until just combined. The filling—of whatever seems best at the moment to go with eggs, or whatever is on hand—can be stirred in with the eggs, but I like to layer it on as a topping before the frittata goes into the oven. I usually put a little salt and pepper over the whole thing rather than in the eggs, for some reason, and often sprinkle a little Parmigiano or shredded Gruyère over it all.

A recipe I can't locate now called for a tablespoon or so of bread crumbs, a like amount of milk, and the zest of a lemon to be mixed into the filling; that's delicious with such combinations as mushrooms and chopped proscuitto, especially with slices of zucchini overlapped in a whirl on top.

FILET MIGNON POULET

One of my favorite dishes is saltimbocca di pollo alla romana from *Italian Cooking in the Grand Tradition*. That recipe must have been on my mind the other night (I had just promised Roger the Vintner to do it for twenty people at a wine-tasting session on Halloween), because I got to thinking, If you can substitute chicken for veal and get a marvelous dish, why can't you run it in for other things? Like wrap bacon around it and do a mock filet mignon?

So I did. You can tell this is a true story, because if it were fiction, wine and Italian cooking and twenty people and Halloween would somehow work with each other to produce a coherent whole, whereas they are merely discrete facts of the sort that drive logical people crazy when they try to make sense out of life. Anyway, what I came up with was nothing like Halloween, but reminded me of the first banquet I ever took a girl to, where they served filet mignon (considerably overdone, though I didn't realize it then) and I stalled until it was dead cold trying to pick up from my neighbors whether I was supposed to eat the bacon or not. As a matter of fact, I still don't know whether you're supposed to or not; but with my chicken filets, yes, you are.

It's a very simple recipe. Just skin, bone, and halve chicken breasts (I do it in the opposite order, really: halve, then bone, then pull away the skin; see p. 178); squeeze some garlic in a press onto the more susceptible side (where the little fillet is, if that doesn't confuse you; opposite the skin side); add a little salt and pepper; fold the ends up and lay them sort of beside each other; wrap a slice of bacon around the sides and force the chicken into a round filet mignon shape, securing it within the bacon with toothpicks.

Brush both surfaces with olive oil or melted butter—plus lemon juice, if you like—then grill for about ten minutes; turn over and grill for another ten minutes or a bit longer, according to whether you prefer your chicken juicy or, as Candy does, dry. I do them on my Weber grill and close the cover when I turn them. They form up very nicely, and they are very tasty.

I served them the other night with a first course of chilled consommé madrilène (see p. 76) garnished with a little twist of roasted red bell pepper (see p. 213). With the main course there was a salad of sliced fresh tomatoes on a leaf of lettuce, topped with cucumber crescents (slices of cucumbers halved lengthwise and seeded with a melon baller, then marinated for several hours in water and vinegar plus a few grinds of black pepper and a few dashes of Tabasco—refrigerated, of course, to keep them crisp), and there were baked potatoes with butter and salt and pepper.

The dinner was good; it would have been a little better if I hadn't got to talking and so forgot to serve the consommé until after the main course and forgot the heated Italian rolls altogether, but it was still good.

For dessert we had vanilla ice cream and cake, but that was because we had it left from Marge's birthday dinner a couple of nights before. What I'd have served otherwise is vanilla ice cream with raspberry syrup and butter cookies. I did, for a change, remember to make after-dinner coffee.

COFFEE

One of my favorite moments of the day is, usually somewhere around sunrise, when I take my first sip of morning coffee. I enjoy all the sips that follow, too.

When I read about the siege of Vicksburg, during the Civil War, it bothers me a lot less that people had to eat mules than that they had to drink the brew of things like roasted acorns instead of coffee.

I have tried all my life to accept things, not to complain, never to rail against fate. That has been my goal through war and sickness, financial crises, humiliation, what have you. But I couldn't help it, when Maurie put me on decaffeinated coffee a few years ago. I didn't just complain: I bitched, for two weeks solid.

"I'm on it, too," Maurie told me at the time. Of course, it was supposedly for our health, and so of course, too, Maurie, being who he is, remarked casually a few days into the ordeal, "You know, don't you, that the stuff they decaffeinate coffee with causes cancer in rats."

So when he and JoAnn and T. J. were here for dinner, and I asked at the end of the meal who wanted coffee, and Maurie raised his hand, and I said, "Okay, decaffeinated for you," and he said, "No. Regular coffee," I drew myself up and said, "Well, by God, if you can have it I can too," and that was the end of that.

My favorite blend is based upon the darkest roast I can get. I didn't spend two years in Louisiana for nothing. How better to solidify your taste for dark strong coffee? After dinner I sometimes use just the espresso roast, but more often I stick with my breakfast blend no matter what time of day—except for my afternoon cup of espresso or cappuccino.

Why I came up with a 9-ounce base for figuring proportions I have no idea, but for 9 ounces water I use just under 1 measure espresso roast coffee, 4 beans Colombian Excelso, 3 beans Mocha Java, and what must be about ½ teaspoon chicory.

I seldom make only 9 ounces, though; in fact, most mornings I make 20, which is difficult to adjust to, or at least to tell anyone how to adjust for: 1 and a little more than ½ measures espresso, 9 beans Colombian Excelso, 7 beans Mocha Java, and about 1 teaspoon chicory.

My thermal carafe supposedly holds 36 ounces, and I make it full for company, sometimes more than once. It takes 40 ounces of water, and I use 3 measures espresso, 18 beans Colombian Excelso, 14 beans Mocha Java, and about 2 teaspoons chicory. Now, does that give an idea?

The ritual is: Heat the cups and the carafe by filling with hot tap water (I keep ours so hot that sometimes guests complain); grind the coffee fine and put it in the gold filter; pour from the kettle into a measuring cup a little boiling water, then pour just enough of that over the grounds to dampen them; let them sit for a brief moment. Empty the carafe of the water that's warming it; set filter with coffee onto it; pour boiling water into the measuring cup—not just to be sure to get the correct amount, but also to cut the temperature of the water back just right—and then onto the grounds. When dripping is complete, stir the coffee, pour a little at a time into your cup, and drink it—slowly, but before it has a chance to cool.

XI

In Spite of All

"On such occasions he would drain a dipper of rum and vichy water and become again the correct English gentleman."

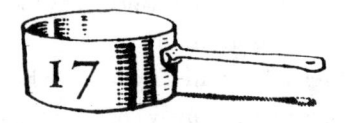

Liver? Never!

Sometimes I wonder if Candy is a scribe translated from ancient Egypt, or perhaps had ancestors that migrated centuries ago from the Lascaux area of France. The other night she had to leave for a soccer game before I got back from teaching a night class, and the note I found was mostly a large drawing of a chicken; "Please don't eat any," was written above it, and below it, "livers."

I *had* been threatening. Sometimes I seize the moment while she's off playing soccer in Canada or somewhere to relieve the freezer of a plastic bagful or so of livers I've stuck back one by one; I either sauté them in butter and deglaze the pan with Madeira or invite temporarily single friends over for bachelor dinners of spaghetti Caruso. The other night, however, I just got out a chunk of leftover lasagne and heated it in the oven. I had forgotten to thaw the chicken livers in advance, for one thing; for another, Candy would soon come limping home—bruised, battered, and still brimming with aggression—into the cooking smells; and for yet another, chorus lines of gamboling pigs in overalls have never whetted my appetite for bacon, and neither does an apparently live chicken, however crudely drawn, set my mouth watering for its inmost parts.

Over the years Candy has restricted our diet not only by fastening upon the one thing she will consider eating for a particular meal but also by having established a sturdy list of what she will not consider, ever. Chicken livers, of course, and calf liver, beef liver, pork liver. Sweetbreads, brains, tripe, chitterlings, or anything that sounds like head, foot, or internal organ. Many if not most vegetables, with Brussels sprouts at the top of the list and green beans not far down the line. Patés, terrines, mousellines, or anything ground up and put back together all soft and pasty. Gravies, sauces, any food in liquid or semiliquid form, or mushy, or pale, or unresistant.

Brun is her mode; never *blanc*. Preferably seared a good rich burnt umber on the grill. Why, then, would she give me a costly copper fish poacher for Christmas a few years ago? Ask her, not me. Since then, we've had quite a number of marvelous fresh whole salmon, flown in from Alaska or somewhere, and although she says she would love a poached fish, no fish in hand turns out to be the one she has in mind. I've cooked every one, by request, with just a little butter and black pepper in the cavity, over charcoal. Well, really, with the coals pulled aside, the fish on aluminum foil, and the Weber closed (but not the holes) for about forty-five minutes, until the skin will pull off easily so that the fish can be laid upon a platter with its flaky pink flesh just waiting to be lifted in savory chunks from the skeleton.

Lots of other things might as well be on her list of Nevers: she doesn't declare them so; she just doesn't eat them. It is perfectly apparent that, regardless of her silence on the subject, lips that touch orange marmalade will never touch hers. I have to admit that I'm pretty much with her there. As a boy, I loved the candied orange peel my mother made about Christmastime, and so I hid away one day with more than I should have snitched and ate myself sick. Until recently I could not look at slivered orange peel without blanching, even though it was seductively suspended in pale amber and tightly sealed in jars.

But Candy doesn't have that excuse, and her range of not-eats covers jams and jellies and preserves, syrups, all varieties of molasses, confitures, conserves, and whatever else people call sweet stuff that you might spread on buttered toast. I made some jelly last fall from the tree that blossoms within a few feet of our deck every spring and then takes on the look of a lady's hat gone berserk with small polished red crab apples. Two of the three batches (one for our neighbors, who let us have the fruit) turned out beautifully. Candy tasted it, pronounced it good, and went back to honey with her morning biscuits.

Honey it is for her, though she still retains an abstract desire for grape jelly. It isn't expressed as an abstract desire, but when we're shopping for things upcoming household guests might want that we don't stock, she'll say, "Might as well get something we'll eat later if they don't," and invariably pick up grape jelly. I thought for years it was a hangover from peanut butter sandwich days, but when I said as much, she bristled. "I have never in my life eaten peanut butter with jelly," she told me. "You eat peanut butter only with plain bread or crackers. Of course, you *can* lick it off the knife."

She has dicta like this about all sorts of things—"Don't eat sausage out, and never eat a hamburger at a swimming pool," for instance—but I didn't want to get into that, so all I said was, "Then where did this lingering notion of grape jelly come from?"

"Oh. Well, I used to spread it on buttered toast, in the morning. And crumble bacon on it. And fold it over. And eat it."

We were driving along in the car a few days later when she volunteered, "Oh, yeah. And with horseradish."

"With horseradish?" I said. "*What* with horseradish?"

"Peanut butter and crackers," she said.

Over the years, Irene and I have snuck some vegetables in on her in a form that she liked—even green beans, when they were fresh from Yarnell's farm up the road. Once we did them three nights in a row in three different ways, and she not only liked them—"Now *these* green beans are good," she said—but ate them. Liking them doesn't always lead to eating them. In fact, she announced after the third night, "All right. Enough. I can do without green beans for quite a long time now, thank you." That was nearly four years ago, and if my memory is correct, she hasn't approved a menu with green beans on it since. We'll have to get Irene back this summer and sneak them in again.

Dried beans have been an area of mild contention, too. A couple of years ago, when I got a hankering to make something with beans in it, I must have read out a couple of dozen recipes while her head went back and forth in a metronomic, all-inclusive negative. Finally, she took over the books. "Here," she said after a spell of turning pages, "if you're determined to do beans, how about this soup?" Since she tends to resist soup, too, I was truly surprised. This one was a very hearty minestrone, with several kinds of greens we don't often see here, and with the beans sort of buried out of notice, which is what I think attracted her.

"Okay," I said somewhat dubiously. "If that's what you want, I'll try to find the ingredients, or fake it a little." I went to several stores; the only way I could find kale was canned; I did find beet tops, as I remember it; for Swiss chard, I mixed some spinach with some lettuce—not the same, of course, but as close as I could come. There was sausage and ham and I don't know what all, too, and I got it all together and spent a day fumbling back and forth between the rather elaborate directions and the cutting board and the pot.

When she stopped eating after the second spoonful, I said, "Now, this was your suggestion, remember?"

"My suggestion?"

"Yes. You picked it out."

"Well, I was just saying that if you wanted to make something out of beans, why not try this soup."

"Exactly," I said.

"I didn't say I wanted to *eat* it."

I didn't say I *didn't* want to eat it, but I didn't. It was too greeny, in the wrong way, and too thick, and too sort of heavy. "Okay," I said, as if it were just as a favor to her, "I'll do some omelettes real quick."

There must have been two and a half gallons of the minestrone. I froze it and tried to think of somebody who might like that sort of thing, but after several months I gave up and, as the garbage truck was halting its way down the street, turned out the solid chunk as a weight on a stack of old newspapers. I could imagine the garbagemen as they tossed it into the huge compactor: "What's *that?*" one of them would say. The other would look at him in disgust: "Minestrone, you idiot."

Black bean soup has always been separated out from Candy's aversion both to beans and to soups. She was sort of knocked out by some she had in a Miami restaurant on her high-school senior trip, on the way to the Bahamas; she ordered it hopefully in other restaurants from time to time afterward and had me try making it off and on, but none quite matched that first, and, of course, she would have none but the best. I gently suggested that maybe, in her youth and naiveté, she had romanticized the moment, that no bean soup in the world would ever equal that first bowl, not even if she were by some miracle allowed, here in her more mature years, that first bowl over again; but Candy is pretty much immune to suggestion.

I tried again just the other day, not to duplicate that mythic Bahama-bound soup, but at least to come up with a formula that we might want to use more than once. I found all the recipes I could, went over them with Candy, then laid out the ones that engaged us both. "You choose," I told her; I'm generally more comfortable with the prospect of putting the blame on her, even if I can seldom make it stick.

"Why don't you sort of combine them?" she said.

So I did. I cooked and stirred all day, planning to have it that night with jalapeño cornbread and what not, for company. When our guests called in sick, we decided to hold the soup for the next night, partly because one recipe said to refrigerate it for twelve hours before warming and serving it. Maybe that day of chilling had something to do with the way it turned out. Candy ate a whole bowl, put down her spoon, sat back, and said, "Well, that's it. You've done it."

"Done it?" I said.

"That's as good as what I had in Miami."

I felt as though I had discovered the Fountain of Youth, although I had never before thought of its waters as being that thick, or as garnished with chopped-up boiled egg and avocado slices and wedges of lime, or, for that matter, as leaving an odd purple stain wherever you spilled it on white Formica.

There is one other soup that Candy likes, in addition to the clear consommé, with shell macaroni and slices of raw carrot, that I make to her specifications. She's always loved vichyssoise, but she can't eat it. We've never figured out why, but it makes her sick every time she tries it. The same ingredients separately or in other combinations don't bother her, but cold or hot, as fancy potato soup they are like poison.

Onions get her, too, unless they are well cooked. She's allergic to them, or something. When we discovered that she really couldn't eat them, I had a brief spell of despair, thinking of all the great dishes I would never get to cook. But it wasn't long before I discovered ways to get around raw onions: sometimes by sautéing them in butter or oil and removing them with a slotted spoon before continuing with the recipe; sometimes by sticking one whole into a big pot dish and removing it whole; mostly by just leaving them out.

Now I tend to react against them myself. I don't get sick, but I find the taste often too strident and too persistent. People who dine with us don't get them and don't miss them, or I'm reasonably sure they don't. I hardly ever put out the salt grinder, since *we* know, of course, that my dishes are well-nigh perfect as they come to the table, and guests have said, "Uh, is the salt here someplace?" But not one has ever demanded, "Where's the raw onion?"

MOCK BAHAMA-BOUND BLACK BEAN SOUP

This is the version I came up with that Candy liked:

1 pound black beans
2 quarts cold water
1 tablespoon lard
2 medium onions, whole
2 cloves garlic, peeled and crushed
1 smoked ham hock
6 green onions (including tops), chopped
2 fresh, mildly hot green chilies, seeded and minced
½ bell pepper, chopped
2 imported bay leaves, crumbled
½ teaspoon salt
½ teaspoon freshly ground black pepper
¼ teaspoon oregano
2 or 3 dashes of Tabasco
1 or 2 tablespoons dry sherry

Put the beans in a heavy pot with the water, then cover and bring to a boil. Add the lard (I was out of lard and used half Crisco and half bacon grease), the two onions, and the garlic; simmer for one and a half hours. Add the ham hock, green onions (these and shallots seem to affect Candy less than big onions do, but even they need to be well cooked), chilies, bell pepper, bay leaves, salt, black pepper, and oregano. Simmer for several hours until beans are tender. Puree the lot in a food processor, and then run it through a food mill. Refrigerate it overnight. Heat it slowly; add the Tabasco and sherry before serving. I used

Slices of avocado

with

Lemon juice
Salt
Freshly ground black pepper

on the side, and with

Chopped hard-boiled egg

to sprinkle on and

Quartered limes

to squeeze over the soup.

SPAGHETTI CARUSO

This recipe makes enough for two hearty eaters.

4 cloves garlic, peeled and crushed
4 tablespoons olive oil
6 tablespoons butter, divided
6 chopped green onions
2 large fresh tomatoes, peeled, seeded, and chopped
1 cup sliced fresh mushrooms
1 cup dry white wine
¼ teaspoon salt
¼ teaspoon freshly ground black pepper
¼ teaspoon dried rosemary
1 pound chicken livers
2 eggs' worth (¾ pound) of fresh pasta (see p. 87), or ½ pound dried
2 tablespoons softened butter
Freshly grated Parmigiano

Heat the garlic in the olive oil and four tablespoons of the butter until it begins to change color; remove with a slotted spoon and discard. Add the green onions and cook over low heat until soft; add tomatoes, mushrooms, white wine, salt, pepper, and rosemary; simmer slowly until thickened a bit. Sauté the chicken livers rather quickly in two tablespoons of the butter until the color changes and they are still pink, but not red, inside. Cook the pasta *al dente* and toss with the softened butter. To serve, mound pasta on a hot platter, top with sauce and then with chicken livers. Pass the Parmigiano.

This is an adaptation of a recipe from *Helen Brown's West Coast Cook Book*. The sauce, which depends very much on good fresh tomatoes, has the same ingredients as recommended there, except that I have doubled the amounts, and instead of chopping the livers and cooking them with the sauce, I leave them whole and sauté them separately. Also, I quadrupled the quantity of livers called for even as I halved the amount of pasta. Does that identify chicken-liver starvation, or what?

Whether this is a way that Caruso would have liked the dish named for him, I do not know. It's the best rendering of it I've ever eaten, in any case.

PASTA with a GUILTY SECRET

If I've failed to mention that Candy hates prunes, it's probably because I've pretty much absorbed her unalterable opinion that prunes are just not things that people like. She's very much about prunes the way my uncle was about opera: I took over some records of arias for my grandmother to hear, when she was living with him, and he reluctantly agreed to let them be played on his phonograph, but only after he was out of the house. "Nobody likes opera," he told the two of us as we sat there waiting to hear some. "*Nobody*. They're just puttin' on."

I don't know why it was that I decided one day to have Candy eat some prunes. I suspect it was because Velma had been here and left some, and I couldn't stand to see them go to waste. In any case, I concocted a pasta dish that we both liked, but that I'll never get by with cooking again.

PASTA WITH PRUNES AND SUN-DRIED TOMATOES

Saute

¼ cup pine nuts

in

2 tablespoons olive oil

till light brown.
Add

1 hot dried red chili, minced
1 hot fresh green chili, minced

and heat till soft.
　Add

4 pitted prunes
An equal amount of San Remo sun-dried tomatoes
A little additional olive oil

Put everything in a Cuisinart and pulse until nearly a paste.
　Cook in boiling water

7 ounces tortellini with cheese filling

Put the tortellini on a hot platter, top with the prune sauce, and top that with

A handful of slivered almonds, toasted

If you're serving to people like Candy, translate it into *tortellini con un segreto colpevole* and trust they don't understand quasi Italian.

PLAID ZUCCHINI

Sometimes if you make things look different they seem to go over better. With Candy, sometimes that means that you hide them altogether, as I did with the prunes. In this case, though, the zucchini is clearly zucchini; she doesn't actively dislike zucchini—it just doesn't engage her.

What I tried to do was, by cosmetic and other means, transmute a rather pale bland wallflower into something of a vamp. If I had achieved that, I probably wouldn't have used plaid in the designation, but, anyway, Candy ate it and liked it.

This is how to do it: Halve lengthwise

1 medium-small zucchini

and scoop out the center with a melon baller.

Chop coarsely together

Scooped-out part of the zucchini
2 Greek Calamata olives
2 Italian oil-cured black olives
A small chunk of Fontina or Havarti cheese

Stuff this into the zucchini halves. Season with

Salt and pepper

Lay on

Julienned bits of pimento

in a pleasing arrangement.

Drizzle with

Olive oil

Sprinkle with

Freshly grated Parmigiano (domestic is fine)

Put under broiler until it looks good.

CHUNKY DRY CHICKEN PIE

This dish was created to satisfy Candy's desire that dishes be totally unwet and unmushy and that they have discrete ingredients.

Just sort of randomly throw into a deep pie dish

Some slices of ham
A couple of chicken breasts, cooked and cut into chunks
Some quartered artichoke hearts sautéed in butter with minced onion (onion removed, if you're so inclined)
2 or 3 hard-boiled eggs, quartered
Some black olives
1 or 2 banana peppers, sliced into circles
At least 1 jalapeño pepper, sliced likewise
What fresh herbs are at hand, chopped
A little stock

Top with a pie crust; cut slits in it with a knife and glaze it with beaten egg yolk and water. Cook in a 350-degree oven until crust is browned; most of the moisture should be evaporated by then. Serves two.

SUPRÊMES de VOLAILLE PEANUT BUTTER and HORSERADISH

One evening not long ago, I asked Candy what she wanted the chicken breasts stuffed with that night (we seem not to have settled that during the day), and she made the mistake of saying, "You're the chef," which left it up to me. Okay, I thought, struck with the memory of peanut butter with horseradish, I'll just give you something I know you like. Somehow, though, as I went furtively about it, chicken didn't seem to equal soda crackers in the combination, so I added bacon. To my surprise, we both liked it. It's not something we want every night; in fact, we haven't eaten it since. But, as a curiosity, at least, marinate in lime juice for at least 20 minutes

2 chicken breasts

Cut a pocket in each and fill with

A thin coating of peanut butter
A thin coating of horseradish
1 slice bacon, cooked crisp

Close pocket, pressing edges together. Season with

Freshly ground black pepper
A light sprinkling of salt

Brush with

1 1/2 tablespoons melted butter
Roughly the same amount of lemon juice

Grill over charcoal, basting when breasts are turned, till chicken is firm and to your taste.

XII

Dénouement

"The Earl started as if shot. 'That name!' he cried, 'that face! that photograph! stop!'"

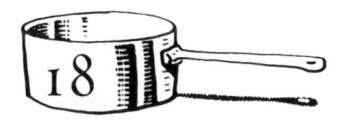

From Mary to Martha

A while back, one of my colleagues told me about a visit to a chronically impatient acquaintance who kept calling out to his wife in another room, "Don't you think it's getting time to eat?" She was in conversation with my colleague's wife and showed no sign of hearing. Finally, the host shouted to her, "Goddamnit, *quit* what you're doing and get out there in the kitchen and *cook*!"

It happened that our good friends Wild Bill and Anne were visiting us when I heard the story, and they and Candy took up the command, directed at me, about every other evening. It wasn't every evening, because when Wild Bill's around, he does the cooking half the time, and when Wild Bill cooks, not only can you count on a top-notch meal but you can count on sitting down to it at eight o'clock.

I don't fully understand it. Wild Bill likes to talk as much as I do. He can sit by the hour and tell stories about his days as a cowboy, or about the time the bears and dogs got into the cabin at the same time and knocked the stove down across the door so nobody could get out. But he has some sort of culinary clock in his head. If he's going to do some of his great chili with the tasty chunks of carefully trimmed beef, he shuts down as raconteur just at the right moment to head for the cutting board and put an edge on the knife.

When it's my turn to cook, I honestly think I'm doing the same thing. I've got this sort of clock ticking away up there as if to say, Just a few more minutes. Just a few more minutes. I'm usually sitting on the couch, drink in hand, trying to get in a story that one of Wild Bill's has reminded me of, but Anne gets one in ahead of me, and then Candy shoves in with one of hers, and by the time I get the prologue of mine out and am ready to launch into the story proper, here comes that chorus of "*Quit* what you're doing and get out there and *cook*."

So I try to give the gist of my story as I back through the dining area into the kitchen and then, despite a general air of inattention, deliver what's left of the punch line across the unlit range top through the hole in the wall before I steal a glance at the kitchen clock with its little hand already edging upward from eight.

There is a story we used to be told in Sunday School about a pair of sisters named Mary and Martha. Mary would sit out with Jesus and the other company and listen; Martha would stay back in the kitchen and cook. Once, though, Martha came out and complained that she did all the work and Mary just visited and never offered to help. The lesson was, as I remember it, that Mary had chosen the better part, and that man does not live by bread alone, and that Martha should quit complaining and get out there in the kitchen and cook.

I certainly didn't question the concept when I was a boy. It practically ordered me to sit with company while my mother and sister fixed dinner. Women were supposed to be back there in the kitchen cooking, anyway, except for the occasional Mary—a little less practical, a little more sensitive in nature—who was allowed to choose the better part. At least, she was allowed to as long as the bread that man doesn't live by alone, but doesn't, of course, live at all without, was getting made by some other woman.

As for Martha, I'm sure the menfolks thought, if they thought about her at all, that she not only wouldn't have been sitting at their feet laughing at their stories but probably would have been trying—she was *just* the type—to get in one of her own.

If Martha had had a hole cut in the wall, she could have kept working in the kitchen and joined in from there. At least, that was the sort of thing I assumed before we had the hole cut in our wall. But although Wild Bill's and Anne's and Candy's voices come through pretty well, as long as the exhaust fan isn't on or I'm not stirring something too heartily, it isn't as easy as I thought it would be to join in from the kitchen side.

The hole seems big enough. It isn't, in fact, so much a hole as a rectangular opening, a sort of window, or something, some four feet long and maybe a foot and a half high, but the way it runs along the range and countertop and comes up just under the cabinets, I sometimes feel like Bottom's Pyramus: "I see a voice. Now will I to the chink, to spy an I can hear my Thisby's face."

You have to bend pretty far over to get anything resembling eye contact with people in the living room; I nearly always manage to bump my head on the metal corner of the vent, but for a long time I didn't let that keep me from trying. "That reminds me," I'd say very loudly, leaning dangerously close to a bubbling pot, but whatever little gap I might have thought I spotted in the conversation would have closed before my bid for attention arrived on the scene.

If I had been convinced that the design of the hole was at fault, I could have set up lunch for good old Jeff, who alters and adds to houses, and gotten plenty of advice over corned beef sandwiches. But it became increasingly apparent that my problem was deeper than carpentry should be expected to cope with. I seemed to have developed overlapping personalities. I had grown up being Mary; I had spent most of my adult life being Mary; I was still trying to be Mary long after I had gone into the kitchen and chosen Martha's as the better part.

Or had I? I doubt that even Martha did, but I certainly have never believed that man lives by bread alone. That's one reason I got speakers for the kitchen and hooked them up to my stereo, so I could have Mozart and Haydn as well as the heft and thump of dough being kneaded. But if all Mary did was sit and listen, that wasn't my idea of a good time, either.

Probably the greatest compliment of my life was that our friend Tom, who is one of the best storytellers alive, once brought his father and mentor, Boots, up to swap stories with me. It must have hurt, but Tom sat back with what I have to think of as unnatural generosity and let just Boots and me have at it. A high point came when, just before the part in his "By Neddy, Skillet" story when Skillet lifts her skirt, Boots leaned his chair back against the wall and said, "Hee, hee, hee. You take it, Tom." It was an all-night session, crammed with some of the best stories I've ever heard, but it wouldn't have been nearly as much fun if I hadn't known through each spell of listening that whatever story I was holding off to tell would be next up.

Every plan I could come up with to be my version of Mary while I was being

Martha had some obvious flaw. Never serving anything that couldn't be stuck in the oven and warmed up? A kind of Pyrrhic solution, since I'd lose all desire to cook. And it just doesn't work to hold off when a story comes upon you; imagine having Candy, when all the food is finally on the table, pick up her napkin and announce, "Now. Let's *all* be quiet and listen to Bob's little joke, or anecdote, or whatever it was he wanted to tell. Go ahead, Bob."

To the noncook it would probably seem simple: Build a huge kitchen and herd in all your company when it's cooking time. But if even a single guest feels sorry for me and comes in to chat, I burn the butter in the roux pan, and forget whether or not I've put in the salt, and discover the tomato aspic still in the refrigerator the next morning.

When it became obvious that I couldn't be Mary-Martha, that I had to choose one or the other, I began to rationalize: You can pretty well count on keeping the attention of a boiled egg you're about to shell, I told myself, even though it may lose little gobs of white despite your best efforts, but one thing you can't count on in this world is holding listeners when you're telling a story. The phone rings. The dog starts barking. A tornado comes up.

That's what happened a couple of years ago when we were visiting our ex-back-fence neighbors Ken and Annie out at their country place. Ken was in the middle of something when Candy said, "I hate to interrupt, but isn't that what a tornado is supposed to sound like?" We all sat a moment listening, and sure enough it sounded just like a train coming. "You have a railroad out here?" I asked Annie. "No," she said. "Well," Candy said, "I think we'd better get to the basement." As we got to the bottom of the stairs, it tore up the tree line behind the house.

I don't think we ever got back to whatever Ken was telling. But in recalling the moment, he and I agreed that we had been hearing the noise before Candy mentioned it. "And all I did," Ken said, "was begin talking louder."

I was once halted in mid-sentence by a fellow raconteur on the porch of a cabin in Louisiana. "I wouldn't break into your story for anything less than this," he said, "but look behind you, down at the end of the porch." It was a lizard of some sort fighting with a huge spider. Eventually the lizard got in a good bite to the body and the spider shriveled up so that we thought he was done for, but the lizard waited until the spider sort of unfolded again and left the scene before he scurried back under a woodpile, and I took up my story again.

Raconteurs usually respect each other's territory, but you can't count on the general public. Well, you can't count on storytellers, either, in a way. They'll steal you blind. I once told a story I'd been telling for years, at a party this time, and my friend the host sidled up behind me and whispered, "You want to hear how that really goes?" He did wait until I had finished; you can't be sure a mere listener will be that considerate.

The worst case of interrupting I could recall—and I used it to help convince myself I was better off with meat and vegetables, anyway, than with people—didn't have to do with telling stories. It happened during my college days, when I was just getting on to opera. One of the coeds, as we called girl students in the post–Rudy Vallee days, begged me to let her hear a new recording of an aria I had been raving about. That Saturday I hitchhiked to her hometown with the highly breakable twelve-inch 78 RPM recording of Jan Peerce, worked for an hour fixing her broken record player, put the record on, and sat back as if to say, Now, listen to *this*, and before the first three bars of introductory music had sounded, her eyes went vague and she said, "Maybe there's something good on the radio."

The fact is that I love to cook, whether people are sitting there waiting or not, and I began to make a deliberate effort to concentrate on that and be just a listener, like Mary, but from Martha's vantage point. From the time I am forced out into the kitchen until I can pull up my chair and rejoin the company, I try to keep my mouth shut and my hands busy. That sounds like something Jesus might have told me to do, if it had been us he visited instead of the sisters, only he'd have put it in a more King Jamesian style, I'm sure.

One result I have noticed is that everybody else seems to finish eating well ahead of me. I suspect that by the time they get to the table they've pretty much said all they have to say, and so while they are replenishing their bodies with what I prepared as Martha, I am left free to enrich their minds with plenty of Mary's not-bread-alone. It is not given everyone to serve his fellow creatures thus.

WILD BILL'S CHILI

One of the things Wild Bill gets out in the kitchen to do in plenty of time for dinner to be on the table at a decent hour is trim. He meticulously cuts off all fat and gristle and membrane until the beef is nothing but lean red meat. That matters. Happily, though, the last time I made this chili, I bought stew beef from Brownie's that was so clean I didn't have to make a single cut or scrape. That should have meant that we sat down to eat no later than 8:30, but as I recall it, something else turned up to slow me down. In any case, this chili, at whatever hour, is good stuff.

In a large pot, sauté till soft

1 large onion, chopped

in

Bacon drippings

Add

A couple of cloves of garlic, chopped fine

Add and brown on all sides

3 pounds good stew meat, trimmed and cut to 1/2-inch dice

Add

About 4 tablespoons good chili powder

Stir good.

Add

2 tablespoons cumin
A big pinch of salt
Some red pepper flakes
1 big (15-ounce) can tomato sauce
A canful of water

Cook over real slow heat a long time. If thickening is needed, add

Masa harina or flour mixed with water

Check taste; add

Cayenne

if not hot enough. A very satisfying meal, with good bread and a salad, for four.

WILD BILL'S POT ROAST

I don't think I ever wrote this down; if so, I can't find it. So maybe I've strayed a little from the original, but the principle is still intact. One thing Bill stresses is to keep the liquid below the meat; this is more a steaming process than a braising.

Into

1 large chuck roast

rub

Several pinches of salt
Lots of freshly ground black pepper
A good sprinkling of cayenne
As much flour as it will take

Brown it all over in

Bacon drippings

Put rack into roasting pan; add, not quite up to rack

2 cups water (or use red wine for $1/2$ to 1 cup)
2 beef bouillon cubes, or 1 cube plus 2 tablespoons meat glaze

Place roast on rack, cover roasting pan, and cook at 350 degrees for several hours—I generally give it five—adding boiling water if the liquid gets too low. The cooked-down juices make an excellent sauce.

TOM'S COUNTRY HAM

The old recipe formula First You Catch the Chicken is applicable here. You do need a really good Kentucky country ham. Tom knows where to get them and how to pick them; I don't. But once you have it, here's what to do with it.

Saw off ham hock, so that ham will fit in pan. Trim off outside fat, leaving a thin layer. Cover top and sides with batter made of

4 cups flour
1 cup dark brown sugar
2 tablespoons dry mustard
2 tablespoons ground cloves
1 tablespoon freshly ground black pepper
Water to make a stiff dough

Bake in oven at 350 degrees for three and a half hours. Remove bone. Cut as thin as possible. Cheese grits goes really well with this.

CHEESE GRITS

Simplify, simplify. We had been not quite happy with one recipe after another for cheese grits until I decided to reduce the dish to its basics—no custardy additions, like eggs or milk. When I tried it, there it was, real cheese grits, come out of hiding.

Bring to a boil

3 cups water
A pinch of salt

Stir in (preferably with a wooden spoon)

¾ cup quick grits

Reduce heat gradually as you stir; cook, stirring, for four or five minutes, until grits are no longer watery and begin to form a mass. Take off heat.

Squeeze into grits with press

1 medium clove garlic

Add

Several grinds of black pepper
A few dashes of Tabasco

Layer in buttered casserole dish

½ the prepared grits
6 ounces shredded sharp cheddar

The remaining prepared grits
6 additional ounces shredded sharp cheddar

Bake in a 350-degree oven for half an hour or so, until heated through and cheese on top is melted and bubbly.

XIII

Coda

"The lovers fell into one another's arms."

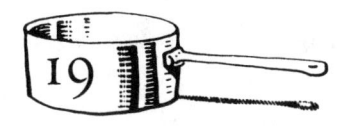

A Womb with a View

One wet summer day not long ago, Candy remarked that since the rain had set in we ought to spend the day on the floor with the Bear. "Good idea," I said. "And we could spread blankets over chairs for tents to crawl into when it thunders." Candy's eyes lit up—but (I note this for those friends who think I'm well into my second childhood and Candy has never left her first) we didn't do it.

We didn't need to. The Bear was already flattened out like a seal under the fortunately large coffee table. Candy had her end of the couch, from which to stretch her feet out onto my end, and a good supply of sports magazines. I had the kitchen.

I had long before taken it over and sort of wrapped it around me, not precisely like a cocoon; I left enough slack for the heaps of living that make a house a home. The first thing I got for the kitchen was a tall wooden stool. My excuse was that it would get me off my feet while peeling potatoes or mincing parsley, but I think I knew that I wouldn't be able to work sitting down. What I really wanted it for was not-working, for those times when everything is clean and put away and I haven't realized that, at my speed, it's already time to start dinner. Just to sit, the way tweedy Englishmen you read about just sit in leather chairs in the library, shut in by untouched books, with fire dying to coals in the grate. Of course, such Englishmen are quickly done in to get a murder mystery under way, but their last few moments must have about them a mindless bliss unmatched outside my kitchen.

Except for me, most of the things that sit about and hang about the kitchen are there because they are useful. Well, my copper is used, and shows it, but I've hung the pots and pans on cabinet doors as much because I like to see them as because there's no other place to put them. The same goes for the copper stock and pasta pots and fish poacher on top of the cabinets, and for the heavy Le Creuset pieces hung from the beams. Perhaps my guests see them as representing my usual step and a half behind American fads, but I see them as timeless, and French. In repose, they give off warmth and solidity; they seem assured that whatever is prepared in them will deserve a Gallic kiss of forefinger and thumb and a *voilà!* rich with satisfaction.

Tony and Becky, my son and daughter-in-law, give us usable kitchen stuff from time to time, like the big wreath of bay leaves, the smaller one of thyme, and the whole batch of marvelous hot red peppers that hang, all of them, untouched and untasted—so pleasant a feast for the eyes and the nose that I have allowed not one leaf, sprig, or pod to lose its life in savoring ours.

The kitchen lights are not just usable, they are necessary—all but one. The fluorescent fixtures over the sink and near the cutting board, the light over the range top, the conical white floods I put in under the cabinets to light up my coffee apparatus and my little Italianate marble area—even during daylight hours I'd have to grope without them. But the handsome ceramic globe hangs from the ceiling because it *looks* good, and because from its terracotta insides it gives out a useless warm, red glow the color of the unglazed tiles of the floor beneath it.

The tiles themselves may be impractical; softer surfaces are available on which to stand for hours and upon which to drop glasses and crockery. We thought, in fact, of a wooden floor, raised to provide both greater resilience and hidden space for running pipes across the kitchen, since the concrete slab on which the house is built doesn't invite new plumbing. But we decided against the awkward step up, step down of a wooden platform, less for practical reasons than because I wanted a solid Mediterranean surface underfoot. That one small patch of tiled floor is the nearest I could come to capturing the feel of my father's birthplace in Sicily, where my cousins walk, as our ancestors did before them, on Palazzo Adriano's cobblestones outdoors, and indoors on stone and marble and tile.

Incongruously, perhaps, a couple or three years ago I took in a television set. I thought I got it because Candy kept yelling from where she was stretched out on the couch, "Hey, come here quick! Rod Carew's stealing home!" Or, "Look! The Pearl River's flooding, and they're showing Mississippi!" Or, "Ha *ha*! There goes Greer Garson again, acting with lips only!" Even if I could leave what I was doing, and even if I enjoyed dashing out into the living room, by the time I got into viewing range, Carew was getting the high five, the news had switched from my home state to Central America, or Greer Garson had stilled her lips to their look of studied composure.

"Maybe I ought to get a little black-and-white set," I said finally. "I could squeeze it in over beyond the Cuisinart, and they only cost fifty bucks or so nowadays."

"No!" Candy said immediately. She is nothing if not decisive. "You deserve color."

Of course, I thought complacently. *Certainly I do*, unaware in my complacency that why I really wanted the TV might have had less to do with baseball and the news and old movies than with complacency itself.

Unborn people and butterflies may be sort of ultimately snug in their cocoons and wombs, but they can't possibly be as *smug* as I can be in my kitchen: They can't, as I can with my full-color electronic window onto what passes for the outside world, intensify their pleasure in being where they are by a view of where they, gratefully, are not. When they do get a glimpse of what's out there, furthermore, they can't push a button and shut it off. And once out, poor things, they can never go back, even when thunder starts crashing all around. On my kitchen stool, I have sat many a time, blank as the little screen off beyond the Cuisinart, and let thoughts like these course through my incipient brain without disturbing in the slightest my foetal tranquillity.

20

La Cucina È Mobile

We knew from our real estate man before we arrived to look at this house that it fit our description of what our Old English sheepdog needed and we wanted. What we hadn't known to ask for was the first thing that caught our eye: we looked through a breezeway out to a deck shaped somewhat like the prow of a ship with a large sugar maple where the mast might be. "We'll take it," Candy said, and we did.

The breezeway is an excellent place for the grill and the smoker; we use them in all sorts of weather, since we can just step out the door and step back in, protected from rain and snow unless it is blowing up a gale. The deck was a great place to sit and have lunch in the shade of the maple, listening to the wind chimes Wild Bill and Anne gave us.

Everything changes, of course. One day Candy found herself ankle deep in the deck, and we realized it was no longer safe for midday habitation. That I could fix. I got a little crowbar, pried out the rotten boards, and put in new ones. The next year, when Candy went through the steps that led down into the side yard (she must put her foot down with more authority than I do; the old wood never gave way with me), I took another look and found that the boards I hadn't replaced were well past retirement age.

I drew up plans, Don, the builder next door, ordered batches of nails, bags of concrete, and a huge stack of treated wood delivered to our yard, and I built a new deck around the maple tree: a larger deck, on two levels. When I got the top part done, I let the Bear come out and help me, which he did by lying quietly and watching, the hair over his hidden eyes lifting and moving expressively as I dug postholes, mixed concrete, worked with the spirit level, measured, measured again, and hauled four-by-four and two-by-six lumber into place. He even learned not to flinch when I nailed beams to posts and sixteen-foot boards atop the beams. When the deck was done, he considered it his; first thing every morning he went out and inspected it.

I wouldn't let anybody else help. Several friends offered me apple cores and things, but unlike Tom Sawyer I wanted no other hand to the work but mine. Louie even volunteered to bring his own hammer; I'd let him come over and cook up a pot of gumbo or crawfish étouffée anytime, but for some reason that deck was mine and the Bear's to build, until finally I did allow Candy, in a rather informal Golden Spike ceremony, to drive the last sixteen-penny nail—whereupon we heard the first thumpings of the groundhogs who moved in, apparently, at the last blow of the hammer.

They kept shoving rocks about where the deck was just above ground, right at the edge of the breezeway. Through the rather uneven spaces between the first two-by-sixes I had put down, we could see some of the rocks and often could see the groundhogs; sometimes their backs pressed against the boards so that their fur poked up into the cracks.

They got very bold. One of them came up onto the deck while Candy was sitting on the glider and the Bear was asleep in the shade of the breezeway. The groundhog paid no attention to Candy, but walked right in front of her toward the Bear. She was afraid the Bear would wake up and they would tangle, so she said (she has a way with animals), "Here, now! Where do you think you're going?"

The groundhog stopped and looked at her.

"Come back here," she told it. "Don't you bother the Bear. This is his deck."

The groundhog turned, looked her right in the eye, and bitched at her in a raspy little voice as he waddled slowly and defiantly within inches of her feet down the length of the deck; he stepped off into the yard, waddled down to the corner, and stood for a while peering through the fence before he squeezed through and headed, apparently, for the creek bottoms.

People had told us that we had to get rid of the groundhogs before they had pups, or little groundpiglets, or whatever their young are called, because some of them would die under there and we'd never get rid of the smell. We decided they were probably right, and took the suggestion that we put out moth crystals rather than the advice that we trap them or shoot them.

It worked. Of course there was a rather long hiatus in our on-deck lunches, since the odor of moth crystals improves the taste neither of pimento cheese nor of corned beef.

Pimento cheese is one of the reasons that Irene tells Candy, "You're in a rut!" on the average of four times a year. She will have dreamed up something new and different for us to try for lunch, and Candy will have said, "I want my pimento cheese sandwich." That's why, on the average of 365 days a year, along about noon I say, "You want your rut?" and Candy says, "Of course."

It's not the same rut every day. When the weather gets cold enough, she switches to grilled cheese. Either is easy to make; the pimento cheese is just sharp cheddar, chopped canned pimentos, and enough homemade mayonnaise to make it spread. Her grilled cheese is simplicity itself: medium sharp cheddar slices in white bread started over high heat in a small pan just as the pat of butter melts; the heat is reduced to medium immediately; when one side of the sandwich is browned, the other side gets its turn in more melted butter. The whole thing has to be pressed throughout the operation with a pancake turner. If it's not squashed flat and very dark, according to Candy, it's not a real grilled cheese sandwich.

I get close to being in a rut at lunch, too. Sometimes I take spells of eating wieners cooked on a ridged iron grill on the range until they are as black as I'd get them over a campfire, two of them in one Thomas's honey wheat English muffin spread with mayonnaise, Pommery mustard on one side, and regular French's mustard on the other side with several drops of Tabasco and sometimes the mild refrigerated kind of sauerkraut wrung as dry as I can get it.

More often recently I've cooked corned beef the way Annabelle at Brownie's Market does it: Rinse it off, wrap it in heavy-duty aluminum foil with a little water, set it in a pan to catch the juices, and put it in a 350-degree oven for two hours. Let it cool, and slice it very thin. It, too, goes well on a wheat English muffin, or on a mild rye bun, but with Dijon mustard instead of French's. Often I put sauerkraut, again as dry as I can wring it out, on one side, topped with either Fontina, Havarti, or Swiss cheese, and the corned beef wadded up on the other, and run it under the broiler until the cheese begins to bubble: a Reuben sandwich, I suppose, or close to it.

When there is leftover prime rib or grilled flank steak or London broil, I slice it very thin and fill my standard wheat English muffin with it, along with mayonnaise, either Pommery or Dijon, Tabasco, and horseradish. Pork loin, left over, is good, too; everything should be sliced as near to paper-thin as it will hold together. The pork is great with a Scottish mustard Candy's Aunt Rudelle gave me some time back, a rather dark, thick substance, containing, as Doctor Johnson would have anticipated and the label confirms, oatmeal.

The deck is just the nearest of the places we take food to eat in the out-of-doors. Sometimes we pack up sandwiches and chips, and a pickle for me, and Candy's fuzzy water (known throughout the rest of the world as Perrier), and my tall brown bottle of Schmidt beer, and a couple of peanut butter cups or Cadbury's chocolate and almond bars, and load our canoe on top of the car; we paddle up Alum Creek until we have had to pull the canoe over five or six shallow little sets of rapids, and then either tie up or get out on a sand-gravel bar and eat.

Other times we take the canoe to an overgrown place, named for the Wyandot chief Leatherlips, on the Scioto River; we take along Candy's fishing rod and, as often as possible, Irene—once with John, during the all-too-brief spell they were married before he died—and cook split bratwursts on the hibachi until they are crisp, upstream from where Candy wades out to cast into the stretch of rocks and rapids near the bank where John named all the wild flowers for us and found deep beds of watercress.

One winter we loaded up a sled with roast beef sandwiches and potato chips and wine and chocolate bars, and a tarpaulin to sit on, and Gary (our Sonny Boy from across the street) and the Bear and Candy and I pulled it down to the creek and onto the island where the Bear loved to sit on the rocks and listen to the shallow riffles, frozen now, and on down to the bare downstream tip, where we had a picnic in the snow.

Not every dish is transportable, of course, not even to places like the family reunions we went to in Standing Pine, Mississippi, when I was a boy, or the dinners-on-the-ground, as we called the tablecloth-covered boards on sawhorses, set up under the oaks in the country churchyards after the preaching was done for the morning on one of the last days of a revival meeting, and loaded with what seemed like all the food in the world. Nobody brought soufflés or baked Alaska, but there are, happily, many good things to eat that do travel.

Nowadays we're less likely to starve ourselves in anticipating such foods through long sermons and interminable verses of final hymns than to tailgate with them before football games. We eat out in the parking lot before at least one game every fall, mostly with our friends Liz and Dave, who know and love good food from both sides of the serving dish. Around us, batches of other fans will be eating and drinking, some off the back hatches of station wagons, some in vans—as we did in Dave's last fall, in a downpour of rain—and some in large groups at folding tables, with bunting and streamers and banners all around, and tapes of the Ohio State marching band blaring from twin speakers. In recent years, the tailgaters have even gone into competition, with the winners announced on the scoreboard during the games.

Whether judges try the food, I don't know. I had my cooking tasted in judgment only once in my life, on one of our rather ragtag Boy Scout campouts. I put the chunk of meat on a stick propped over the fire through the Y of a limb stuck into the ground, and buried the potato in the coals, as directed, but the fire died out while I was gone to the spring for drinking water.

When the scoutmaster came around, the potato I handed him was warm, but still hard. I waited for his snort of disgust, but what he cut off and tasted, it turned out, was the only bite that got done. He did the same thing with the meat. I don't know how; it was much too dark to distinguish cooked from uncooked. Maybe he could divine it, the way a preacher I knew claimed he could wave a fork over a chicken pie, poke through the crust, and pull out the gizzard—and did just that the only time I saw him try.

Anyway, I had passed the taste test, but the second phase was to eat what you had supposedly cooked. I did manage to choke it down, but if there had been anything else to put in my stomach before spreading a blanket on the rough ground and trying all night to get some sleep, I would gladly have flung my meal into the brush for whatever local animals might appreciate it, and let the merit badge for cooking go hang.

Competitive tailgaters have no conception of such primitive goings-on, and even we, as their more private and unpretentious neighbors, are sybaritic compared to my first experience with outdoor consumption. I always cook the eggs, for instance, before halving them and mashing up the yellows with mayonnaise, salt, white pepper, and either a little curry powder or dill weed or, for my favorite kind of stuffed eggs, cut-up bits of Greek Calamata and Italian oil-cured black olives—sometimes with minced San Remo sun-dried tomatoes and a little juice from a jar of green olives. A slice of pimento-filled olive looks good on top.

I nearly overcook—we like them crisp—little balls of Brownie's excellent bulk sausage, touched up with hot red pepper flakes. That could have been one of the batch of things we loaded into the car on Pep and Polly's wedding anniversary a few years ago and served as appetizers during the drive to a distant restaurant for dinner. Another was green olives coated with cream cheese and rolled in finely-chopped walnuts. It was all Irene's idea, of course, including our present of fluted champagne glasses, which, from the back seat, she presented to them filled, as an overcome Pep alongside her muttered a bit wildly, "This is a di*sas*ter! This is a di*sas*ter!"

I don't remember whether we had some sort of sandwiches then, but some I often make for tailgating are kin to the coated olives we did have: They are made with cream cheese (4 ounces) and chopped pimento-stuffed olives (¼ cup) and chopped walnuts (2 tablespoons), with a little cream to smooth it all out and a dash or two of Tabasco, spread on thin slices of substantial white bread. Along with those, in our parking-lot feasts, fried chicken legs are great (soaked for half an hour in brine with ice cubes, dried, tossed in a sack with flour, salt, black pepper, paprika, and cayenne, and fried in a couple of inches of Crisco or oil heated to 375 degrees). David must be related to Irene; even though our excursion is casual and our fare more practical than elegant, he always insists on bringing champagne.

My favorite eater-out at football games was even a notch less formal than we. He was a little man who used to come to the games with his professor son and grown grandchildren. For a couple of years our seats were right behind his. We knew he was Italian when he opened up one of the paper grocery bags he had lugged in and started handing out fresh plum tomatoes, the motion of his hand so eloquently urging his progeny to eat that I could hear my Sicilian relatives saying it in chorus: *"Mangia! Mangia!"*

The paper bags would keep yielding up bread, salami, grapes, apples. Eventually, he would take out his thermos and pour a cup of red wine as if it were coffee. By halftime he would be talking to everybody within earshot, turning back to me and even the people behind me to say, "I don' like Pittsburgh. I *hate* Pittsburgh. Pittsburgh stinks." Soon he would slump down into silence, apparently lapsing, despite the roar of ninety thousand football fans, toward the *riposo* that the food and wine, the sunny afternoon, and his Mediterranean blood inevitably blended into.

HAMBURGERS

My most recent foray into Europe was so long ago that there was, as far as I observed, only one hamburger joint in existence there at the time, a Wimpy's in London. Now, I understand, they're all over, converting foreigners and catering to American tourists' craving for the most ubiquitous and prolific sandwich, whether grilled at home or eaten out, in these United States. The craving seems to get stronger the farther we get from American beef and American buns, but it's strong enough here at home. It seems to grow in Candy and me at the same rate; we'll go along for anywhere from two weeks to a month on a diet of everything but, and then simultaneously our heads will swivel toward each other and we'll say, virtually in chorus, "You ready for hamburgers tonight?"

The buns we use are the same Thomas's honey wheat English muffins we use for nearly all sandwiches. Candy likes hers with only a thin coating of mayonnaise on one side and Dijon mustard on the other—too dry for my taste. I use a fairly heavy spread of mayonnaise on each side, with Dijon added on one and just enough catsup on the other to make Candy say, "Wipe your beard," two or three times per hamburger. I also like thinly sliced dill pickles pretty well coating the meat.

I make for the two of us three patties, fairly round and not too thick, out of a pound of Brownie's ground chuck; since Candy will eat only one hamburger, I make hers a bit larger than the two I make for myself. A quick grind of salt and a few grinds of black pepper go on each side, and enough Worcestershire on one side barely to color the meat. The coals should be very hot, so that the first side sears and browns up richly in almost no time. When the hamburgers are turned, the lid of the Weber goes on, with holes open: We like rare beef, but the flavor of hamburgers is enhanced, it seems to us, if the meat is quite pink inside, and warm, but not red. You learn to feel the right moment to take them off; when you press them with the turner, they have taken on a sort of determined coherence without getting in the least hard. If the bottoms have not browned sufficiently at this point, remove the top of the Weber and let the coals heat up enough to sear them.

SKEWERING

We enjoy chunks of beef or chicken marinated and/or basted and grilled over charcoal on skewers, but there is nearly always a problem when you put vegetables in between. They *look* good; before they're cooked they are nearly as pretty as the cooked ones in books and magazines that seem to have been photographed in some Disney world instead of the flawed one we live in. But some of the vegetables cook before the meat is done and sort of hang limp, and a marinade strong enough for the meat is generally too strong for the vegetables.

One obvious solution is to put the meat on one set of skewers and the vegetables on another, so that you can set them over the coals at different times. That takes away from the picturesque alternation of colors and textures, but it often eats better.

The solution to the flavor problem is just as obvious: Don't use the same marinade for the vegetables as you use for the meat. There are thousands of recipes for meat marinades (for beef, I suggest the ingredients for Bob's roast, modified, using gin instead of bourbon—see p. 112), but since I've run across few for vegetables, I came up with one of my own. It brings out zucchini, especially, better than anything else we've tried.

VEGETABLE MARINADE

Combine

2 parts olive oil
2 parts lemon juice
1 part dry vermouth
Lots of freshly ground black pepper

Marinate whatever vegetables you choose—cut to fit on a skewer, of course—for as long as you like, refrigerated to hold their crispness. Skewer them loosely and baste with the marinade as you grill.

CHICKEN MARINADE

A good marinade for chicken is only slightly stronger—the same ingredients to a point, with a touch more heat and a touch more bite. Cut boned and skinned chicken breasts into roughly one-inch cubes and, for half an hour or more, marinate in

4 parts olive oil
4 parts lemon juice
4 parts dry vermouth
1 part Dijon mustard
A few dashes of Tabasco
Several grinds of black pepper

Skewer the chicken pieces loosely and baste with the marinade as you grill.

LOUIE'S CHICKEN and ANDOUILLE GUMBO

You don't generally think of gumbo as a traveling food, but Louie's gumbo and his étouffée have been known to travel from his kitchen to other places, including mine. Not only that, but there is a history of mobility behind his Cajun cooking. He is a native of Ohio but with French Canadian ancestry, which may be why when he went to Louisiana he was so taken with the French Canadians who long ago were transported there from Acadia and developed into Cajuns. When he returned to Ohio, he brought back not only a Louisiana French wife but also a tasty portion of their cuisine.

Andouille (rhymes, he says, with chop suey) is a Cajun sausage made with chopped, instead of ground, meat, very savory. Since it is not readily available here, smoked sausage can be used in its place, but it's not the same, and Louie has been known to have batches of andouille shipped up. Once the people at the bus station called him to say that he had a package he should pick up immediately. They had put it outside, certain that it was going bad—but that's just the way andouille smells.

Gumbo is typical Cajun food, Louie says, in that it's a one-pot dish that starts with a roux and uses whatever is at hand. In fact, he says, no matter what recipe you ask for in the family of Carole, his wife, the response begins, "First you make a roux," although they make so much at a time that generally a batch is waiting in the refrigerator to be heated up. Cajun food is still, despite its recent popularity, often confused with the fancier Creole cuisine, and certainly with overly seasoned blackened everything. "Cajuns," Louie says, "don't burn their food."

First, then, we'll make lots of roux (or cut the recipe down to suit yourself) and then assume that what's at hand is chicken and andouille—not likely but you're lucky if that happens to be the case.

LOTS OF ROUX

Stir together

>   2 *cups cooking oil*
>   2 *cups flour*

over medium heat until dark.

THE GUMBO

To

>   6 *tablespoons hot roux*

add

>   *1 or 2 cut-up chickens, skinned*

Seasoned with

>   *Red pepper flakes*
>   *Freshly ground black pepper*
>   *Salt*

Cook till chicken has given off its juices, stirring so that it won't stick. The juices and roux will combine and build up a startling amount of gravy.

Add

>   *1 pound andouille or smoked sausage, sliced*
>   *2 medium onions, chopped*
>   *¾ green bell pepper, chopped*
>   *3 stalks celery, chopped*

and cook till tender.

Add

1 large can chicken broth
1 can or more hot water

till chicken is covered and then some.
Cook over low heat until done. Add

Filé

in individual servings, not in the pot. Serve over rice. Feeds four to eight, according to the number of chickens and the size of the appetite.

Filé is ground sassafras root, and it is fairly easy to come by, even here. If added to the pot, it strings out like egg white.

RICE

Use twice the volume of water as of rice, plus a dollop of margarine. Bring the water to a boil, add rice, stir, cover, and cook over low heat for twenty minutes. This sort of splits the rice and makes it mushy. That's the way they do it.

LOUIE'S CRAWFISH ÉTOUFFÉE

Louie has had crawfish shipped up, too. They just don't seem to be as plentiful in Ohio waters as they are in Louisiana. Shrimp can be used instead; it's not the same, but it's still good.

Season

2 pounds peeled crawfish tails (or shrimp)

with

Salt and freshly ground black pepper

and set aside.

Melt in a heavy pot

1/4 pound Imperial margarine (or use oil)

Add

1/2 cup celery, chopped
3 to 4 cups onions, chopped
1/2 cup bell pepper, chopped

and cook, stirring, till onions are wilted.

Add

2 tablespoons crawfish fat (yes, crawfish fat; elaboration follows)
1 1/2 cups water
Crawfish tails (or shrimp), above

Bring to a boil and cook over slow heat for thirty minutes, stirring occasionally.

Dissolve

2 teaspoons cornstarch

in

½ cup water

and add to crawfish mixture.
Add

¼ cup onion tops and parsley, chopped

and cook another ten minutes.
Season with

Salt
Freshly ground black pepper
Red pepper flakes

Serve over rice. Enough for four.

Crawfish fat is the part that you get when you break off the tails and "suck the heads." It's the yellow stuff with the crawfish tails you buy frozen. If you get tails without fat, use the fat stuff of your choice. That's what you have to do, anyway, with shrimp.

XIV

Silver Lining

"The Earl was killed in the hunting-field a few days later. The Countess was struck by lightning. The two children fell down a well. Thus the happiness of Gertrude and Ronald was complete."

21

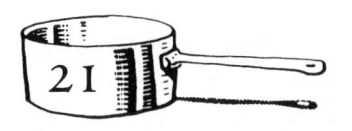

Where Does It All Go?

These chapters were written over a period of several years. For a while I kept going back to the first ones and bringing them up to date, but I began to realize that there had to be a cutoff point or I'd be at this forever. A good many things have changed, the kitchen among them; it has given up the globe light in favor of track lighting, for one thing, so that I can see what I am doing. My convection oven quit working and gave me an excuse for trying a microwave; so far I use it mostly for thawing and warming (it's great for restoring frozen sandwich-sized portions of corned beef or thinly sliced leftover roast to just the right temperature). Cookbooks have nudged out even the potatoes Anna pan, and I have about a dozen waiting for shelf space; decision time must come soon.

The tree in whose shade we so often had our lunch went gradually into what plant physiologists pinpointed as Maple Decline; it has left an unfilled hole in our deck and in our lives, but it did go out through the fireplace, keeping the living room bright and warm a couple of winters ago. The dear old Bear is gone, too, the victim of a heart problem; one unnaturally warm February day he started off as he did every Sunday (how he knew the days of the week we never quite understood)—pulling us right instead of left at the end of the street and on around the block for his weekly visit with Marge—but he didn't quite make it all the way.

Irene flew in from Dallas with a clutch of baskets to gather us up in, or we might not have survived. The Bear can never be replaced, of course, but the very next Sunday Candy held in one hand a puppy just exactly a week old, another Old English sheepdog, marked so much like the Bear as eventually to confuse people. His tiny nose was pink, at that stage, and just reached the ends of her fingers. We visited him every Sunday until he came to live with us at seven weeks and became our Topper, soon as large and black-nosed and irreplaceable as the Bear.

Mornings we walk with Topper, as we did with Bear, through the woods and along the banks of Alum Creek, watching for deer and ducks, great blue herons, red-tailed hawks, an occasional owl being pestered by cawing ravens, groundhogs, muskrats, and the kingfisher chittering away as he dives and swoops headlong down the surface of the stream.

Friends have moved out and in—Dave and Liz to Florida, Fifi back from Boston too late to get into this account. New ones have cropped up: Jim, who refers to me as an appliance pig but recently had his kitchen done over and an appliance garage (that's what the contractor called it) built in. Other men cooks, too—Hugh, who prepared an elegant meal for us and, as he sat to serve, announced in a stricken voice, "I just realized that everything I've fixed is carbohydrates"; Dana, who made his debut as a tamale slave, helping Fifi soak ojas, then spreading them with masa.

That's a story for a later time. When I met Irene at the airport just before New Year's Eve, her carry-on bag felt like lead. It was something decidedly more interesting—the ingredients for a belated Mexican Christmas tamale-making. I told her then, as I sagged to starboard along the corridors, that she'd given me the first sentence of my next book: "Irene arrived with twelve pounds of masa." Next day, Tom arrived with a Horse Cave, Kentucky, country ham.

When Brownie sold his market and retired, Don, who bought it, kept it comfortably the same until his venture into another store failed and forced him to give up both. The next owners never seemed to understand the concept of Brownie's; before long, creditors moved in and closed it for good.

Second-rate food and huge impersonal supermarkets with parking lots as big as Kansas had begun to threaten me with Cuisine Decline when Don came to the rescue. Exactly eleven days, twenty-three hours, and thirteen minutes ago, he opened Brownie's again: There behind the meat counter stood Annabelle and Betty and Jean, with John at the cutting board; Polly and Nancy were at the cash registers again, Ray tending to produce, and Don toting sacks of good Brownie's stuff out to people's cars between forays to the rear to see that things were running smoothly. I have missed only one day going there since the store reopened, but plan to go twice next Saturday.

As I look back over what has happened since I got myself hooked up with the kitchen, a question keeps asking itself: "So where does it all go, the food we eat and the times we have together?" Don't expect me to get profound. I tried once, on my fortieth birthday—stayed up alone to sit and look into the fire and think profound thoughts; after a blank half hour I gave up and went to bed. Anyway, the answer my frittering brain comes up with is, "Into the Great Maw of Existence," but if that tells us something I don't know what it is.

An hour or so ago when I had my first taste of morning coffee, with its aroma steaming up into my face, I felt that I could dwell in that moment forever. If I could have, I would never have arrived at this moment: It is not yet sunrise, but the air is bright outside my window with the heavy, wet snow that has just fallen clinging to every branch and twig. My daughter, Nina, is here for a visit, and soon Topper will see to it that she and Candy wake up so that we can take our walk in the creek bottoms on this, his fourth birthday. I know that I can't hold this moment, either, but memory and anticipation make that pretty much beside the point, don't they?

INDEX

Albino spaghetti, 134–35
Appetizers
  crabmeat Justine, 51–52
  green olives with cream cheese and walnuts, 269
  sausage balls, 268
  stuffed eggs, 268
Artichoke bottoms, 78
Augusta National quiche, 200–201

Barbecue
  Ken's Chinese ribs, 114–15
  ribs, 158–59
  pork shoulder, 159–60
  pork sandwiches, 159–60
  sauce, 160
Beans
  green, 140
  baked, Candy's, 163–64
  black bean soup, 234–35
Beef
  bourguignon, 32–34
  chili, Wild Bill's, 252–53
  corned beef sandwiches, 266
  hamburgers, 270–71
  leftover, sandwiches, 266
  mochomos, 211–12
  pot roast, Wild Bill's, 254
  roast, Bob's, modified, 112–13
  steaks, grilled, 8
  Stroganoff Irene, 30–31

Black bean soup, mock Bahama-bound, 234–35
Bloody Marys, 49–50
Bob's roast, modified, 112–13
Bratwursts, 267
Bread
  cornbread, 141
  freezing, 20
  French, 20–22
  Mom's rolls, 131–33
  tortillas, flour, 211–12
Brown roux, Cajun style, 275

Cajun-style rice, 276
Candy's baked beans, 163–64
Cannelloni, 9–11
Celery soup, cold, 180–81
Cheese
  grits, 256–57
  grilled sandwich, 266
  pimento, 266
  soufflé, 196–97
Chicken
  and andouille gumbo, Louie's, 274–76
  breasts
    boning, 178–79
    filet mignon poulet, 223–24
    suprêmes de volaille à la bordelaise, 77–78
    suprêmes de volaille en papillote, 173–77

suprêmes de volaille peanut butter and horseradish, 243–44
legs, fried, 269
livers, 229
  spaghetti Caruso, 236–37
pie, chunky dry, 242
skewered, 273
  marinade, 273
Chili sauces, 209–10
Chili, Wild Bill's, 252–53
Chilled consommé Madrilène, 76, 224
Chinese mustard, 115
Chunky dry chicken pie, 242
Coffee, 225–26
Cold celery soup, 180–81
Collards, 140
Confusion Blossoms in the New Year, 64–65
Consommé Madrilène, chilled, 76, 224
Cookies, 142
Cornbread, 141
Corned beef sandwiches, 266
Crabmeat Justine, 51–52
Crawfish étouffée, Louie's, 277–78
Cream cheese and olive sandwiches, 269
Cucumber crescents, 224

Desserts
  cookies, 142
  ginger snaps, Grandmomma's, 142–44
  ice cream, 116
    chocolate with nuts, 117–18
    coffee, 118–19
    tangerine sorbet, 214–15
    vanilla, 82
  pie
    lemon meringue, 145–147
    peach, deep-dish, 127
  pêches Melba, 81–82

Drinks
  Bloody Marys, 49–50

Eggs, 193–94
  omelettes; see Omelettes
  quiche; see Quiche
  separating, 193
  soufflés; see Soufflés
  storing, 193–94
  stuffed, 268

Fettucine Alfredo, 89–90
Field peas, 140
Fig preserves, 136–37
Filet mignon poulet, 223–24
Fish
  salmon, whole grilled, 230
French bread, 20–21
  freezing, 20
Fresh tomato pizza, 12–13
Fried chicken legs, 269
Frittatas, 222

Gazpacho, 208–9
Ginger snaps, Grandmomma's, 142–44
Greek-like salad, 79–80
Green beans, 140
Green olives with cream cheese and walnuts, 269
Green salad, 79
Grilled cheese sandwiches, 266
Grits, cheese, 256–57
Guacamole, 211
Gumbo, Louie's chicken and andouille, 274–76

Ham, Tom's country, 255
Hamburgers, 270–71
Hollandaise sauce, 28–29
  Edith's, 35

Index

Ice cream, 116–17
  chocolate with nuts, 117–18
  coffee, 118–19
  tangerine sorbet, 214–15
  vanilla, 82

Jewels of Mei Tang Poo, 62–63

Ken's Chinese barbecued ribs, 114–15

Lasagne Padre Giovanni, 99–102
Leftover beef sandwiches, 266
Leftover pork loin sandwiches, 266–67
Lemon meringue pie, Mom's, 145–47
Louie's chicken and andouille gumbo, 274–76
Louie's crawfish étouffée, 277–78

Mandarin salad, Velma's, 80
Marge's tomato juice, 48
Mayonnaise, 189–92
Meat glaze, 171
Mexican food, 208
Mexican rice, 212–13
Mrs. Mary Bobo's slaw, modified, 161–62
Mochomos, 211–12
Mock Bahama-bound black bean soup, 234–35
Mom's lemon meringue pie, 145–47
Mom's rolls, 131–33
Mustard, Chinese, 115

Nopales, 213–14

Olive oil, 134
Olives, green, with cream cheese and walnuts, 269
Omelettes, 221–22
  frittatas, 222
  Monica's, 222
Onions, 233

Pasta
  cannelloni, 9–11
  fettucine Alfredo, 89–90
  impressionista, 91–92
  lasagne Padre Giovanni, 99–102
  making, 87–88
    by hand, 87
    in food processor, 88
  ravioli, 97–98
    attachment, 85–86
  spaghetti, albino, 134–35
  spaghetti Balduini, 95–96
  spaghetti carbonara, 94
  spaghetti Caruso, 236–37
  spaghetti San Remo, 93
  with prunes and sun-dried tomatoes, 238–39
Peach pie, deep-dish, 127
peas, field, 140
Pêches Melba, 81–82
Pie
  chunky dry chicken, 242
  lemon meringue, Mom's, 145–47
  peach, deep-dish, 127
Pimento cheese sandwiches, 266
Pizza
  crust, 13
  fresh tomato, 12–13
  spicy, 13–14
Plaid zucchini, 240–241
Pork
  barbecue sandwiches with sauce, 159–60
  ham, Tom's country, 255
  leftover loin sandwiches, 266–67
  ribs, Ken's Chinese barbecued, 114–15; barbecue, 158–59
  sausage balls, 268
  pork shoulder, 158–59
Pot roast, Wild Bill's, 254
Potatoes, baked, 8
  on the half shell, 138

Index

Poultry. *See* Chicken; Rock Cornish game hens with pine nut stuffing

Quiche
    Augusta National, 200–201
    Irene, 198–99

Raspberry syrup, 82
Ravioli, 97–98
    attachment, 85–86
Rice
    Mexican, 212–13
    Cajun style, 276
Roast, Bob's modified, 112–13
    Wild Bill's pot, 254
Rock Cornish game hens with pine nut stuffing, 53–54
Rolls, Mom's, 131–33
Roux, brown, Cajun style, 275

Salad dressings
    for Greek-like salad, 79–80
    for Mandarin salad, 80
    for slaw, 161–62
    vinaigrette, 79
Salade verte, 79
Salad
    Greek-like, 79–80
    green, 79
    Mandarin, Velma's, 80
    salade verte, 79
    slaw, Mrs. Mary Bobo's, modified, 161–62
Salmon, whole grilled, 230
Salsa verde, 210
Sandwiches
    barbecue, 159–60
    corned beef, 266
    cream cheese and olive, 269
    grilled cheese, 266
    hamburgers, 270–71
    leftover beef, 266
    leftover pork loin, 266–67
    pimento cheese, 266
    wieners, 266
Sauces
    barbecue, 160
    chili, 209–10
    guacamole, 211
    hollandaise, 28–29, 35
    mayonnaise, 189–92
    salsa verde, 210
Sausage balls, 268
Seafood
    crabmeat Justine, 51–52
Skewered vegetables, 272–73
    marinade, 272–73
Slaw, Mrs. Mary Bobo's, modified, 161–62
Soufflés, 195–97
    cheese, 196–97
Soup
    black bean, 234–35
    from stock, 180
    chilled consommé Madrilène, 76, 224
    cold celery, 180–81
    gazpacho, 208–9
Spaghetti
    albino, 134–35
    Balduini, 95–96
    carbonara, 94
    Caruso, 236–37
    San Remo, 93
Spicy pizza, 13–14
Spinach, 10–11
Steaks, grilled, 8
Stir-fries
    Confusion Blossoms in the New Year, 64–65
    Jewels of Mei Tang Poo, 62–63
    stir-frying, 59–61
Stock, 170–71

Stuffed eggs, 268
Suprêmes de volaille
  à la bordelaise, 77–78
  en papillote, 173–77
  peanut butter and horseradish, 243–44

Tangerine sorbet, 214–15
Tomatoes, 12
  juice, 48
Tom's country ham, 255
Tortillas, flour, 211–12
Turnip greens, 139–40

Vanilla, 119
Vegetables
  artichoke bottoms, 78
  beans, green, 140
    baked, Candy's, 163–64
    black bean soup, 234–35
  celery soup, cold, 180–81
  collards, 140
  cucumber crescents, 224
  gazpacho, 208–9
  in hot oil, 18
  nopales, 213–14
  onions, 233
  peas, field, 140
  potatoes, baked, 8
    on the half shell, 138
    skewered, 272–73
      marinade, 272–73
  spinach, 10–11
  tomatoes, 12
    juice, 48
  turnip greens, 139–40
  zucchini, plaid, 240–41
    skewered, 272–73
Velma's Mandarin salad, 80

Wieners, 266
Wild Bill's chili, 252–53
Wild Bill's pot roast, 254
Wine, 75

Zucchini, plaid, 240–41
  skewered, 272–73

Design by David Bullen
Typeset in Mergenthaler Garamond #3
with Centaur/Arrighi display
by Wilsted & Taylor
Printed by Maple-Vail
on acid-free paper